W9-BNO-292

Physical Characteristics of the West Highland White Terrier
(from the American Kennel Club standard)

Body: Compact and of good substance. Chest very deep and extending to the elbows, with breadth in proportion to the size of the dog. Loin short, broad and strong.

Tail: Relatively short, with good substance, and shaped like a carrot. It is covered with hard hair without feather, as straight as possible, carried gaily.

Coat: Must be double-coated. The outer coat consists of straight hard white hair, about 2 inches long, with shorter coat on neck and shoulders. The ideal coat is hard, straight and white.

Hindquarters: Thighs are very muscular, well angulated, not set wide apart, with hocks well bent, short, and parallel when viewed from the rear. Rear legs are muscular and relatively short and sinewy.

Color: The color is white, as defined by the breed's name.

Size: The ideal size is 11 inches at the withers for dogs and 10 inches for bitches.

West Highland White Terrier

By Penelope Ruggles-Smythe

Contents

KENNEL CLUB BOOKS: **WEST HIGHLAND WHITE TERRIER**
ISBN: 1-59378-213-6

Copyright © 2003, **2005** • Kennel Club Books, LLC
308 Main Street, Allenhurst, NJ 07711 USA
Cover Design Patented: US 6,435,559 B2 • Printed in South Korea

All rights reserved. No part of this book may be reproduced in any form, by photostat, scanner, microfilm, xerography or any other means, or incorporated into any information retrieval system, electronic or mechanical, without the written permission of the copyright owner.

10 9 8 7 6 5 4 3

Photography by Isabelle Français, Carol Ann Johnson and Antonio Philppe, with additional photographs by:

Norvia Behling, Carolina Biological Supply, Liza Clancy, Kent and Donna Dannen, Doskocil, James Hayden-Yoav, James R. Hayden, RBP, Dwight R. Kuhn, Dr. Dennis Kunkel, Nancy Liquori, Alice Pantfoeder, Mikki Pet Products, Phototake, Jean Claude Revy, Dr. Andrew Spielman, Nikki Sussman, Karen Taylor, Alice van Kempen and C. James Webb.

Illustrations by Renée Low.

The publisher wishes to thank all of the owners of the dogs featured in this book, including Vera Agnello, Doug and Joan Calhoun, Philippe Coppe, Natalie Cuccioli and Maryse Delaye.

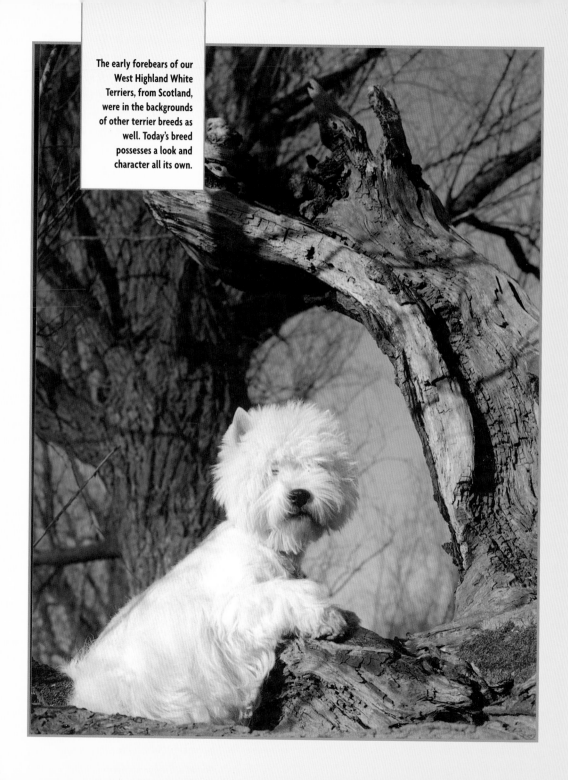

The early forebears of our West Highland White Terriers, from Scotland, were in the backgrounds of other terrier breeds as well. Today's breed possesses a look and character all its own.

HISTORY OF THE
WEST HIGHLAND WHITE TERRIER

MEET THE WEST HIGHLAND WHITE TERRIER

The West Highland White Terrier! His name says much. A terrier, therefore a breed of earth dog. White! A white dog, neither black, brown nor brindle. And he hails from the West Highlands, surely the little fellow is from Scotland, where the countryside is rugged, the brogues thick and the dogs courageous.

This book will give you the history, characteristics and description of the Westie. You will also learn about puppy care, training and the health of the breed. In the color photographs, you will see that the Westie is cute as a button and a wonderful companion. This may not be the dog for everyone, as terriers are active, busy dogs and this breed has a white coat to keep up. However, if you like a plucky, lively dog, one that will be a devoted family member, this may be the dog for you. And, as is true with most other breeds, once you give your heart and home to a Westie, you will remain a devotee to the breed for a lifetime.

An early representative of the West Highland White Terrier, Eng. Ch. Placemore Prosperity, owned by Mrs. Allow.

HISTORY OF THE WHITE TERRIER

In the history of dogs, the West Highland White Terrier is not an ancient breed; however, its official

A DELICATE BALANCE

Since dogs have been inbred for centuries, their physical and mental characteristics are constantly being changed to suit man's desires for hunting, retrieving, scenting, guarding and warming their master's laps. During the past 150 years, dogs have been judged according to physical characteristics as well as functional abilities. Few breeds can boast a genuine balance between physique, working ability and temperament.

terriers fell roughly into two basic categories: the rough-coated, short-legged dogs of Scotland and the longer legged, smooth-coated dogs of England.

The family of Scotch Terriers—those bred in Scotland—divide themselves into the modern Scottish Terrier, the West Highland White Terrier, the Cairn Terrier and the Skye Terrier. In the early 1800s, dogs referred to as the Scotch Terrier could be any of the first three breeds mentioned. Interbreeding was common among

Three typical representatives of early Westies from the original Scottish stock: Col. Malcolm's Boidheach, the Countess of Aberdeen's Eng. Ch. Cromar Snowflake and Col. Malcolm's Doichioll II.

beginnings, which trace back to the late 1800s, place it among one of the older breeds recognized in the world of pure-bred dogs.

The West Highland White Terrier belongs to the group of dogs known as terriers, from the Latin word *terra,* meaning *earth.* The terrier is a dog that has been bred to work beneath the ground to drive out small and large vermin, rodents and other animals that can be a nuisance to country living.

All of the dogs in the Terrier Group originated in the British Isles with the notable exception of the Miniature Schnauzer, which derived from Germany. Many of the terrier breeds were derived from a similar ancestor and, as recently as the mid-1800s, the

these breeds and all three breed types could come from the same litter.

As breeders started exhibiting at dog shows, it was realized that there must be more uniformity within the breed, i.e., all pups in a litter should look alike as well as be of the same type as their sire and dam.

The Westie's history is better known than the background of some of the other terriers, where the history is often a bit murky and convoluted. In the early 1800s, the Malcolm family of Poltalloch in Argyllshire kept a group of small white dogs. As with all terrier breeders, these dogs were bred for working and not for the show ring. "Unless they were fit and game for the purpose, their heads were not kept long out of the huge butt of water in the stable yard." Those who bred and kept dogs had a specific purpose of work for their

At the turn of the 20th century, Eng. Ch. Brean Glunyiema, owned by Mrs. Innes, was considered an ideal Westie of the day.

particular dog—long legs for speed, short legs for going to ground double coats for protection against the elements, etc.

It is written that the Malcolm clan preferred the white terrier due to a hunting accident in which their favorite sandy-colored dog was mistaken for a fox and shot. After that, they kept only cream or white terriers for breeding. While some breeders of terriers destroyed their white puppies, as they felt that they were not as hardy as the colored dogs, the Malcolms felt that the white dogs were as courageous and feisty as the colored ones and proved that the white dog was as able a terrier as any other.

In the mid-1800s, there were other strains of white terriers, in the Highlands. The Roseneath, bred by gamekeeper George Duke, who was on the staff of the Argyll estates, is in the background of the Cairn Terrier. The Pittenweem Terrier, which was regarded as the

TOP SHOW WESTIES

Prestigious wins by the West Highland White Terrier: Ch. Wolvey Pattern of Edgerstoune, owned by Marion Eppley, was Best in Show at Westminster Kennel Club in New York City in 1942. Barbara Worcester Keenan's Ch. Elfinbrook Simon was Best in Show at Westminster in 1962. Ch. Ardenrun Andsome of Purston, owned by Dr. Alvaro Hunt, was Best in Show at the Montgomery County Kennel Club's all-terrier show in the U.S. in 1976. Mrs. K. Newstead's Eng. Ch. Dianthus Buttons won Best in Show at Crufts in England in 1976. Derek and Joan Tattersall's Eng. Ch. Olac Moonpilot was Best in Show at Crufts in 1990.

The term Scotch Terrier could refer to any of the terriers of Scotland, the family of dogs to which the Scottish Terrier belongs.

Designed to pursue badgers and otters, the Sealyham Terrier was created in the mid-1900s. The West Highland White Terrier is believed to have been used in the creation of the Sealyham Terrier.

varminty look about them. They are very active, with a linty-white type of coat, and well-knit together. The coat is hard and bristly, from an inch to two and a half inches in length except on the head and muzzle where it is short, hard and wiry. The head is long, nose broad, the teeth extremely large for so small a dog. The ears are pricked and covered in a short velvety coat. The tail is well-set, slightly curved and carried gaily. I have had the breed and know what they are fit for and may add that no water was ever too cold and no earth ever too deep for them." The same description fits the breed quite well today.

In the early dog shows, terriers were often shown under the classification of Scotch Terriers and often there would be quite a variety of types in this class. In 1904 the Scottish Kennel Club held the first class for the West Highland White

White Scottish Terrier, was a strain that died out fairly early. Sir Malcolm did not care for either the Roseneaths or the Pittenweems and refused to allow any of his dogs to be crossed with these strains. The Poltalloch dogs of the Malcolms were the white strain that moved forward, bred true and became the foundation of the modern breed. Colonel Sir Ian Malcolm, with his white Poltalloch Terriers, is considered to be the father of the breed, in addition to having given the breed its official name, the West Highland White Terrier.

An early description of these terriers was written by a Captain Mackie and published in *Gray's Dogs of Scotland* in 1891: "The Poltalloch Whites weighs from 16–20 lb. with a determined

The Cairn Terrier, also of Scotland, differs from today's West Highland White Terrier in color and structure, to an extent.

Terrier and in the same year the West Highland White Terrier Club of Scotland was founded with the Duke of Argyll serving as the first president.

In 1907 the first championship for the breed was won and 141 Westies were registered in Scotland. In the same year Crufts held classes for the breed and the West Highland White Terrier Club of England was formed. The breed grew rapidly after this and, prior to World War I, 3,947 Westies had been registered and 27 became champions of record.

Some early prominent names in the breed were Holland Buckley and his daughter of the Scotia Kennels, Mrs. B. Lucas of the Highclere Kennels and Mrs. Cyril (May) Pacey of the Wolvey Kennels. The Wolvey Kennels became very well known and eventually produced an impressive 58 champions. By 1916, all dog shows ceased in the British Isles with the onset of World War I. Breeding was greatly curtailed because of the difficulty in finding food due to the strict food-rationing laws. Many breeders had

Col. Malcolm's
Sonny and Sarah
were typical of the
Westie during the
early days of the
breed's develop-
ment.

to put down dogs and Mrs. Pacey herself had to destroy 15 dogs. Most breeders tried to retain a few

dogs in order to keep going, and breeding was allowed again in 1919. By 1920, dog shows resumed and five championships were won that year.

Mrs. Pacey continued her excellent breeding program and at the time of her death in 1963, 25% of all recorded champions carried the Wolvey prefix. She was well known as a breeder and many of her dogs found their way to the Scandinavian countries as well as to other Continental countries.

Many outstanding dogs were bred between 1920 and 1940 in England and it was also during this period that professional handlers started showing Westies.

CANINE DERIVATION

Dogs and wolves are members of the genus *Canis*. Wolves are known scientifically as *Canis lupus* while dogs are known as *Canis domesticus*. Dogs and wolves are known to interbreed. The term canine derives from the Latin derived word *Canis*. The term *dog* has no scientific basis but has been used for thousands of years. The origin of the word *dog* has never been authoritatively ascertained.

The handlers, with their expertise with the stripping knife, started smartening up the little dogs. Owner-handlers followed suit with their grooming in order to keep up with the competition and the Westie eventually took on a "smart" look rather than the prior "working" look that the breed had in its earlier years.

CROSSING THE ATLANTIC
WESTIES IN THE UNITED STATES

In the early 1900s the white dogs that had been brought to the United States were registered as Roseneath Terriers and, in 1906, five were entered at the Westminster Kennel Club dog show under that classification.

Virginia Murray is generally credited with bringing the first West Highland White Terrier to the United States in 1907, and she became a dominant force in the breed for many years. In 1909 the breed was recognized by the American Kennel Club, and the West Highland White Terrier Club of America was admitted to AKC membership in September of that year.

The United States has always had a very dedicated group of Westie fanciers who not only have bred a number of fine Westies but also have imported top dogs from England who have won top

> ### THE WHITE SCOTTIE
> Contrary to what many believe, ("Is that a white or a black Scottie?") the two dogs on the Scotch bottle are the Scottish Terrier and the West Highland White Terrier. The Scottie has a long muzzle with longer ears placed high on his head; the Westie has a short, broad muzzle with smaller ears. The Scottish Terrier is a much heavier boned and heavier bodied dog than is the Westie.

honors at the shows. More importantly, these English imports have produced American offspring who have continued to do well in the ring and for breeding programs.

In the late 1920s, Edgerstoune Kennels, owned by Mrs. John Winant (later Mrs. Marion Eppley), thrived until the 1950s, producing over 40 champions.

The famous drawing by Sir Edwin Landseer (1839), showing a West Highland White Terrier along with other sporting dogs.

In the 1920s a famous German breeder, Mrs. Binzwanger, brought the West Highland White Terrier to southern Germany (Bavaria) where they were successful in ratting. She showed her dogs regularly at German dog shows.

Mrs. Eppley imported many fine dogs from England, including the great Ch. Wolvey Pattern of Edgerstoune. John Marvin noted in his book *The Complete West Highland White Terrier* that Mrs. Eppley had "an astute ability to pick a winner at home or abroad." Some years ago, she judged a show in England and placed a Westie bitch Best in Show. Immediately after the judging, she bought the bitch and brought her back to America. The acquisition was Ch. Wolvey Pattern of Edgerstoune, who went Best in Show at Westminster (1942).

Years later, the same situation was repeated. Again in England, Mrs. Eppley placed a Scottish Terrier Best in Show and then bought the dog. Ch. Walsing Winning Trick of Edgerstoune emulated Pattern and also gained the pinnacle at Westminster (1950).

Mrs. John Marvin bred three Best in Show Westies, a wonderful accomplishment for any breeder, and she has been active in the dog show scene for over half a century. Her husband John Marvin was a well-known terrier writer and both Marvins were judges of many breeds. John and Bea loved England and made yearly trips to the British Isles, watching the judging, looking over the dogs, searching out dog books and visiting with their many friends.

Wishing Well Kennels, started by Mrs. Florence Worcester and her daughter Barbara Keenan, began about 1950. Barbara purchased her first Westie at the age of 13 from Mrs. Winant of Edgerstoune Kennels. In 1954, she imported Ch. Cruben Dexter, who became a leading sire as well as a Best in Show dog. Her import, Ch. Elfinbrook Simon, not fully appreciated in his home country, went Best in Show at Westminster in 1962 and added 26 more Bests in Show to his name in addition to being an influence as a sire in the breed. Dogs and bitches from this kennel have been a force in the Westie world in America for many years. Mrs. Keenan is also a very well-known judge.

Naomi and Jim Eberhardt were active breeders and exhibitors for many years. They have had approximately 75 American Westie champions and have been active in the breed club, and both judge numerous breeds. Many years ago I attended my first Montgomery County show in Pennsylvania and the weather was very cold and wet. (I have since learned that these can be the prevalent weather conditions for this show, similar to most of the shows in England.) Mr. Eberhardt gave me some wonderful little handwarmers that campers used. I put them in my pocket and thought that he had saved my day, in addition to probably saving my life! Of course, I admired Mr. Eberhardt

Miss Genevieve Tobin, a famous movie star of her day, and her smiling West Highland White Terrier named Punch. Miss Tobin was very influential in the popularization of the breed.

for having these clever devices and for being smart enough to bring them to a dog show.

There have been many active breeders of Westies in America, and books authored by John Marvin and Anna Katherine Nicholas give extensive history of the breed in the U.S.

WESTIES IN CANADA
In Canada the first Westie registered was a bitch in 1909. Victor Blochin, Bencruachan Kennels, owned the first group-winning Westie in Canada. He bred from the 1930s to the 1950s and his dogs are found in the

---

PROOF IN OIL
Records dating back to James I (1566–1675) note that he requested that "6 little white earth dogs from Argyllshire be sent to the King of France as a gift." Are these the ancestors of the modern Westie? Sir Edwin Landseer's "Dignity and Impudence," 1839, shows a hound and a small white terrier that is undoubtedly a West Highland White Terrier.

A West Highland White bitch and her puppies, photographed in the 1920s. Note the considerable similarities in type between this dam and many of today's Westies.

background of many Canadian kennels, including the kennel of Mrs. J. H. Daniell-Jenkins.

Mr. and Mrs. Daniell-Jenkins' Kennels of The Rouge was a very active kennel, founded in 1948. Mrs. Jenkins worked closely with Mrs. B. G. Frame of the Wiston Kennels. She was a very busy and popular dog show judge throughout North America, where an exhibitor always knew that she would look over the dog competently and carefully. She passed away in 1992.

Penny-Belle Scorer has had Westies for most of her life. Mrs.

Mrs. Pacey was famous for her Wolvey Kennel, which produced a very uniform variety of Westie. This photograph was taken in 1909, in the first decade of the breed.

A group of the Poltalloch dogs of Col. Malcolm. From these dogs derive most of the West Highland White Terriers in the world today!

West Highland White Terrier puppies born in America about 1920. The breed grew in popularity on both sides of the Atlantic.

Daniell-Jenkins invited her for a visit to see the Kennels of The Rouge Westies and later Penny-Belle became a member of the West Highland White Terrier Club of England under the auspices of Mrs. Jenkins. Her first import was Ch. Arnholme Almost an Angel, who has more than 20 champion descendants. Her Can. and Am. Ch. Biljon Bisbee finished his title in one week and became Canada's #2 Westie and #5 Terrier in 1984. In 1985, she imported Brierlaw Blaze a Trail, who became #1 Westie in Canada in 1986, 1987 and 1988. He not only earned his Canadian championship but also added American and Bermuda championships to his name.

WESTIES AROUND THE WORLD

Westies were first shown in Australia in 1964. During the 1960s dogs were imported from England, including some Wolvey dogs. Australia has a group of dedicated breeders with good dogs and the future of the breed "Down Under" is in good hands.

Westies have become popular in the Scandinavian countries also. Barbro Eklund introduced Westies to her Swedish kennel of Scottish Terriers. In 1962, Birgitta Hasselgren bought her first Westie from Mrs. Eklund and this was

A FAMILY DIVIDED

The Cairn Terrier and the West Highland White Terrier closely resemble each other. The early Cairn breeders were very careful not to keep Cairn puppies that had any white in their coats and any puppies that did have white were culled at birth.

On the other hand, the breeders of the white terriers made certain that their dogs were completely white. Interbreeding of the two breeds continued until 1917 when the American Kennel Club stated that no Cairn could be registered if there was a Westie cross within the first three generations. The Kennel Club of England followed suit shortly after.

Almost 100 years ago West Highland Whites and Cairns were used almost exclusively in Scotland as rodent killers. Their owner, Miss Ransford, credited these three hunters with killing 101 rats in six nights!

Westies have been in Finland since the 1930s but the breed became very popular in the 1980s with membership in the Westie club growing to over 400. In the 1960s, Ch. Wolvey Proton was imported by Marita Palmo and her name appears in many pedigrees, even up to the 1980s. Registrations reached record numbers in the 1970s but registrations began to decline in the 1980s. Once again in the 1990s, the breed flourished with many active and dedicated breeders.

the start of the Tweed Kennels. Her Eng. and Swed. Ch. Tweed Tartan Caledonia has sired many Swedish and English champions. Louise Westerberg from Smash Kennels has also produced top winners. Swed. Ch. Smash Scallyway was #3 Terrier in 1989. Swed. Ch. Smash Turbo was the #1 Westie in 1991 and a multiple Best in Show winner.

In Norway, the first Westie was imported from England in 1931. In 1984, Olac Moon Falcon was imported and became a multiple group and Best in Show winner. The Norwegian Westie Club, an unofficial club, has over 175 members and well over 200 registrations. Although the

West Highland White Terriers are vivacious and intelligent, as is confirmed by the expressions on the faces of these dogs.

numbers are still small, the breed is increasing in popularity.

Derek Tattersall, of the very successful Olac Kennels in England, has an interest in the breed in the Scandinavian countries and has written in depth about this in his book *Westies Today*.

The Westie, in less than 100 years, has become a very beloved breed throughout the world. It continues to be in good hands from North America to the

Today's Westie has found many other uses for his talents. Agility trials have been popular for many years and are becoming widespread around the world.

Continent of Australia. England continues to be its home but top dogs are now coming from around the world.

From their origins in Scotland about a century ago, today's handsome West Highland White Terrier has become recognized and adored around the world.

If you are Scottish, you'll know what this is all about. Scottish clans have regular annual outings during which they sport their traditional garb and show off their national dogs.

CHARACTERISTICS OF THE

WEST HIGHLAND WHITE TERRIER

The Westie is a wonderful little dog! He's cute, apartment-sized, filled with personality-plus and very active. Some terriers, like the Westie, are "below the knee" in size, but in spite of their size, all terriers are masculine dogs and do not show any sign of timidity or shyness. These are busy dogs, on their toes and ready for action! If you are looking for a sedentary lap dog, this will not be the breed for you.

The Westie has a very steady disposition and fits in well with family life, whether it be in a large country house or an apartment in the city. He gets along well with children and will accept strangers once he has had a chance to become acquainted. He's a cocky dog who may not go out and start a fight but he will surely stand his ground when pushed. This is not a dog that will lie about the house trying to keep his master or mistress happy. He has been bred as a hunter, a dog to go after vermin, and he can be ready to work instantly.

Common characteristics for all terriers are their desire to work with great enthusiasm and their courage. They all have large and powerful teeth for the size of their bodies; they have keen hearing and excellent eyesight. No matter for how many generations they have been pets, the purpose for which the breed was bred will remain with the dog.

The Westie is similar to his Scottish counterparts, the Scottish Terrier and the Cairn Terrier. Of the three, the Scottie is the most substantial dog, the heaviest in weight, the largest in bone and the

Most Westies today live in pet homes, keeping their owners warm and happy.

To own a Westie is to own responsibilities. This is a smart dog that wants his mistress to be his equal.

most dour in personality. The Cairn is the lightweight of the group, being a small-boned and lightly built animal. The Westie is nicely placed between these two breeds, in substance and personality. He has substantial bone but weighs less than the Scottie. He likes to have a good time but he is steady in his personality. He likes to please his keepers and has a happy outlook on life. Take a look at a Westie and you can see the sparkle in his eye that says, "Come play with me!" He is a quick, alert and intelligent dog who likes his owner to be his equal.

If you are a first-time dog owner, you must be aware of your

MUTUAL THERAPY

Do you want to live longer? If you like to volunteer, it is wonderful if you can take your Westie to a nursing home once a week for several hours. The elder community loves to have a dog to visit with and often your dog will bring a bit of companionship to someone who is either lonely or who may be somewhat detached from the world. You will not only be bringing happiness to someone else, but you will be keeping your little dog busy—and we haven't even mentioned the fact that it has been discovered that volunteering helps to increase your longevity!

responsibility toward your new friend. Either keep your dog on a leash or in your fenced yard. Your Westie, if loose and trotting along at your side, will spot a squirrel across a busy street and dart after it, never minding the traffic. Therefore, some rudimentary obedience training should be in line so your pal will sit when asked to, come when called and, in general, act like a little gentleman.

Westies, as with other terriers, can be a challenge in the obedience ring. Terriers are not easy breeds to work with in obedience. Their intelligence and independent spirit can sometimes be more trying to train than most owners anticipate. You will see

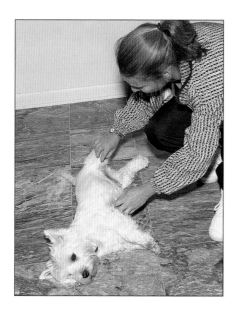

First, there is the problem of a white dog. White dogs will show the wear and tear of their busy lives. Scotties, with their dark coats, and Cairns, with their mottled coats, can run up and down the yard and, when you bring them in, you may not be aware of just how soiled their coats may be. The Westie, on the other hand, particularly if he has been digging, which terriers are prone to do, will truly look a sight as he runs through the door on your clean kitchen floor. If it is a wet and muddy day, he will look even more frightful. Grooming, a requirement in all breeds, is essential in the Westie if you want a dog that you can live with.

Second, there are health problems in most breeds of dog and the West Highland White Terrier is

Westies love to be petted. It is not unusual that they will lie on their backs and expose their soft underbelly to be scratched. This is the ultimate posture of submission.

Golden Retrievers, Poodles and Miniature Schnauzers in abundance in obedience classes as these are breeds that are easy to work with. Not only are they intelligent but, more importantly, they have a willingness to please their master, a quality that is less abundant in the terrier breeds.

The terrier is easily distracted and busy but he is an intelligent dog and he does respond to training. Of course, when training a smart and independent dog, the handler will often learn humility while the dog is learning his sits and stays.

As desirable as the Westie sounds, do be aware when purchasing this breed that there are some problems that you would not have in other breeds.

BREEDERS' SUPPORT

The Westie Foundation of America, Inc. is an arm of the West Highland White Terrier Club of America. This is a foundation supported by the national club, its regional clubs and its membership. Financial assistance is given for medical research of health problems in the Westie. Findings will help breeders of Westies throughout the world and will give all the hope that some of the breed's health problems will eventually be eliminated.

A responsible owner must learn about the possible problems that Westies encounter and what can be done to safeguard his or her pet.

no exception. The new Westie owner should be aware of these problems. Do remember to buy your puppy from a reputable breeder and ask the breeder if any of these health problems are in his line.

Legge-Calve-Perthes disease (Perthes) is a bone-related disease that affects short-legged terriers as well as humans. This is not a hereditary disease and it is thought to be caused by an injury or possibly a nutritional problem. The disease appears between four

Youngsters must learn to properly hold and play with the Westie puppy. Vets suggest that many physical problems can be caused by improper handling.

and ten months and is very painful. The dog will limp on one or both rear legs and eventually the leg muscles become wasted. There are some treatments for Perthes that should be discussed with your veterinarian.

Craniomandibular osteopathy (CMO) is a fairly rare disease found in Westies, Scotties and Cairns. It is apparently a hereditary disease although the exact pattern of inheritance is not known. This is a calcification of the joint

between the lower jaw and the skull, a multiplication in growth of bone cells. It usually occurs between four and seven months and it must not be confused with a teething problem or with cancer. Puppies who have this disease will

SKIN PROBLEMS

Eczema and dermatitis are skin problems that occur in many breeds and they can often be a tricky problem to solve. Frequent bathing of the dog will remove skin oils and will cause the problem to worsen. Allergies to food or something in the environment can also cause the problem. Consider trying homeopathic remedies in addition to seeing your veterinarian for direction.

have difficulty in opening their mouths. Diagnosis is made by x-ray, and cortisone and homoeopathic remedies have been used with good results. This is a very painful disease for the dog.

Copper toxicosis is a serious problem in the Bedlington Terrier and has been found in some bloodlines in Westies. Affected animals develop hepatitis and eventually liver cirrhosis. Considerable studies and testing have been done on this problem and researchers have found that the disease is caused by an autosomal recessive gene that results in faulty copper excretion from the liver. Reputable breeders will have their dogs tested and will not breed affected dogs.

Keratoconjunctivitis sicca (dry eye) is a problem that was noticed in Westies in the early 1980s. This

is not a common problem in the breed, but it has been reported and owners and breeders should be aware of it. It is a recurrent form of conjunctivitis that becomes chronic and very painful for the dog. The problem can be treated with drugs that will increase the secretion of tears but this is not a long-term solution.

Although this list of health problems may look daunting, the Westie is still considered to be a healthy breed. The problems mentioned are present in the breed and a buyer should be aware of them. Some of these diseases are rare and most of them only turn up on the rare occasion. Do not be turned away from the breed but do be aware that if the breeder of your puppy is reputable, he will be doing his utmost to keep them out of his line.

Westies are usually happy, healthy dogs that make great pets. They should, however, be taken to a vet every year for a general physical examination. Many maladies, if detected and treated early, can be successfully cured.

WORKING TRIALS FOR TERRIERS

The American Working Terrier Association offers a Certificate of Gameness at sanctioned trials. A dog must enter a 10-foot-long tunnel buried in the ground, which includes one right-angle turn. Once in the tunnel, he must reach his prey in 30 seconds. Working Trials are held throughout the country and open to all terriers.

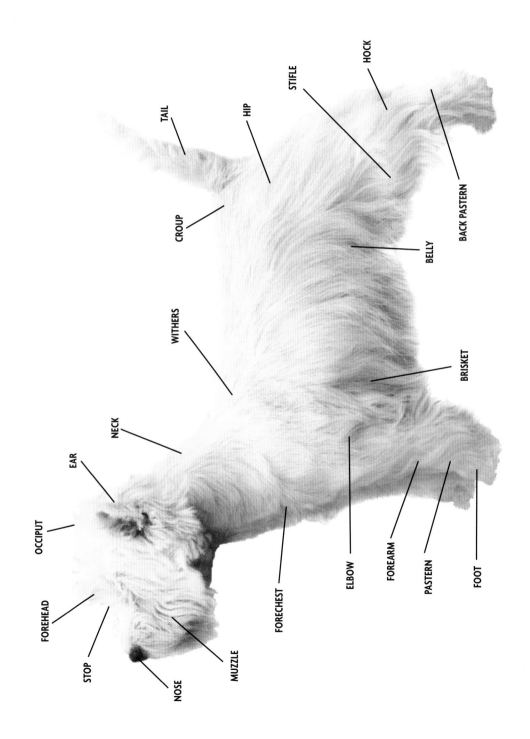

TAIL

HIP

STIFLE

HOCK

CROUP

BACK PASTERN

BELLY

WITHERS

BRISKET

NECK

EAR

OCCIPUT

FOREHEAD

STOP

NOSE

MUZZLE

FORECHEST

ELBOW

FOREARM

PASTERN

FOOT

WEST HIGHLAND WHITE TERRIER

Each breed approved by the American Kennel Club has a standard that gives the reader a mental picture of what the specific breed should look like. All reputable breeders strive to produce animals that will meet the requirements of the standard. Most breeds were developed for a specific purpose, i.e., hunting, retrieving, going to ground, coursing, guarding, herding, etc. The terriers were all bred to go to ground and to pursue vermin.

In addition to having dogs that look like proper West Highland White Terriers, the standard assures that the Westie will have the personality, disposition and intelligence that are sought after in the breed.

Standards were originally written by fanciers who had a love and a concern for the breed. They knew that the essential characteristics of the West Highland White Terrier were

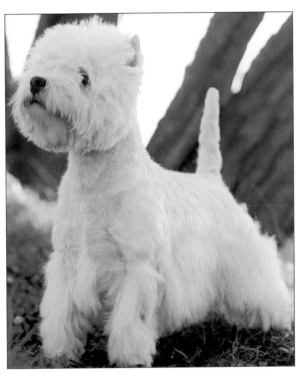

West Highland White Terriers, like many breeds, have evolved over the years. Compared to early representatives of the breed, today's Westies are more refined and impressive.

unlike any other breed and that care must be taken that these characteristics be maintained through the generations.

As time progressed and breeders became more aware that certain areas of the dog needed a better description or more definition, breeders would meet together and work out a new standard. However, standards for

Many points in a breed standard are subject to interpretation. In the Westie standard, there can be no discussion of the breed's color: white.

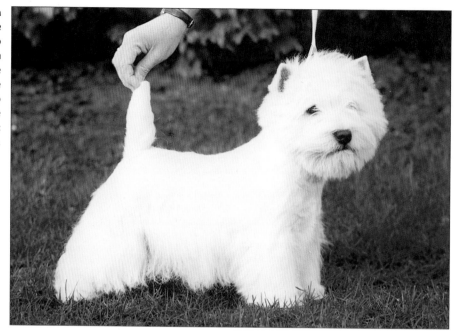

any breed are never changed on a whim and serious study and exchange between breeders takes place before any move is made. Following is an excerpt from the AKC standard.

THE AMERICAN KENNEL CLUB STANDARD FOR THE WEST HIGHLAND WHITE TERRIER

General Appearance: The West Highland White Terrier is a small, game, well-balanced, hardy looking terrier, exhibiting good showmanship, possessed with no small amount of self-esteem, strongly built, deep in chest and back ribs, with a straight back and powerful hindquarters on muscular legs, and exhibiting in marked degree a great combination of strength and activity. The coat is about 2 inches long, white in color, hard, with plenty of soft undercoat. The dog should be neatly presented, the longer coat on the back and sides, trimmed to blend into the shorter neck and shoulder coat. Considerable hair is left around the head to act as a frame for the face to yield a typical Westie expression.

Size, Proportion, Substance: The ideal size is 11 inches at the withers for dogs and 10 inches for bitches. A slight deviation is acceptable. The Westie is a compact dog, with good balance

This lovely West Highland White Terrier is a group winner from Ireland. What a fine specimen and a handsome coat!

The correct head on the West Highland White Terrier imparts the breed with a distinctive look. The breed should appear absolutely alert, courageous and gay.

sharp and intelligent. Looking from under heavy eyebrows, they give a piercing look. Eye rims are black. Ears—Small, carried tightly erect, set wide apart, on the top outer edge of the skull. They terminate in a sharp point, and must never be cropped. The hair on the ears is trimmed short and is smooth and velvety, free of fringe at the tips.

and substance. The body between the withers and the root of the tail is slightly shorter than the height at the withers. Short-coupled and well boned.

Head: Shaped to present a round appearance from the front. Should be in proportion to the body. Expression—Piercing, inquisitive, pert. Eyes—Widely set apart, medium in size, almond shaped, dark brown in color, deep set,

Skull—Broad, slightly longer than the muzzle, not flat on top but slightly domed between the ears. It gradually tapers to the eyes. There is a defined stop, eyebrows are heavy. Muzzle—Blunt, slightly shorter than the skull, powerful and gradually tapering to the nose, which is large and black. The jaws are level and powerful. Lip pigment is black. Bite—The teeth are large for the size of the dog. A tight scissors bite with

HEAD
The head is slightly domed. The distance from occiput to eyes is slightly greater than the length of the foreface.

EARS
The ears should be small, erect and pointed (left). They should not be rounded and set too wide apart (right).

BACK AND NECK
The back is level and the shoulder should slope backwards (left). The neck is sufficiently long but never exaggerated as shown on the right.

HINDQUARTERS
The hocks are bent and well set in under the body (left). Weak hocks and cow hocks (turning inward) are undesirable (right).

FOREQUARTERS
The forelegs are straight and muscular (left), never turning out at the elbows (right).

upper incisors slightly overlapping the lower incisors or level mouth is equally acceptable.

Neck, Topline, Body: Neck—Muscular and well set on sloping shoulders. The length of neck should be in proportion to the remainder of the dog. Topline—Flat and level, both standing and moving. Body—Compact and of good substance. Chest very deep and extending to the elbows, with breadth in proportion to the size of the dog. Loin short, broad and strong. Tail—Relatively short, with good substance, and shaped like a carrot. The tail is never docked.

Forequarter: Shoulder blades are well laid back and well knit at the backbone. Legs—Forelegs are muscular and well boned, relatively short, but with sufficient length to set the dog up so as not to be too close to the ground. The legs are reasonably straight, and thickly covered with short hard hair. Feet—Forefeet are larger than the hind ones, are round, proportionate in size, strong, thickly padded; they may properly be turned out slightly. Dewclaws may be removed.

Hindquarter: Thighs are very muscular, well angulated, not set wide apart, with hock well bent, short, and parallel when viewed from the rear. Legs—Rear legs are muscular and relatively short and sinewy.

Coat: Very important and seldom seen to perfection. Must be double-coated. The head is shaped by plucking the hair, to present the round appearance. The outer coat consists of straight hard white hair, about 2 inches long, with shorter coat on neck and shoulders, properly blended and trimmed to blend shorter areas into furnishings, which are longer on stomach and legs. The ideal coat is hard, straight and white, but a hard straight coat which may have some wheaten tipping is preferable to a white fluffy or soft coat. Furnishings may be somewhat softer and longer but should never give the appearance of fluff.

Color: The color is white, as defined by the breed's name.

Gait: Free, straight and easy all around. It is a distinctive gait, not stilted, but powerful, with reach and drive. In front the leg is freely extended forward by the shoulder. The hind movement is free, strong and fairly close. The hocks are freely flexed and drawn close under the body, so that when moving off the foot the body is thrown or pushed forward with some force.

Temperament: Alert, gay, courageous and self-reliant, but friendly.

Dogs like the West Highland White Terrier are bred to preserve their physical characteristics, described in the breed standard, as well as such intangible properties as personality and temperament.

WEST HIGHLAND WHITE TERRIER

WHERE TO BEGIN

If you are convinced that the West Highland White Terrier is the ideal dog for you, it's time to learn about where to find a puppy and what to look for. Locating a litter of Westies should not present a problem for the new owner. You should inquire about breeders in your area who enjoy a good reputation in the breed. You are looking for an established breeder with outstanding dog ethics and a strong commitment to the breed. New owners should have as many questions as they have doubts. An established breeder is indeed the one to answer your four million questions and make you comfortable with your choice

The price you pay for a puppy is usually related to the quality of the parents. Puppies bred from champion West Highland White Terriers have the best potential to be closest to the breed standard.

of the West Highland White Terrier. An established breeder will sell you a puppy at a fair price if, and only if, the breeder determines that you are a suitable, worthy owner of his dogs. An established breeder can be relied upon for advice, no matter what time of day or night. A reputable breeder will accept a puppy back, without questions, should you decide that this is not the right dog for you.

When choosing a breeder, reputation is much more important than convenience of location. Do not be overly impressed by breeders who run brag advertisements in dog magazines about their stupendous champions and

When observing a litter of West Highland White Terrier puppies, select a puppy that is animated and affectionate. Never feel sorry for the puppies that shy away from you.

concern of considerable importance. Since the West Highland White Terrier's temperament can vary from dog to dog, socialization is the first and best way to encourage a proper, stable personality.

Choosing a breeder is an important first step in dog ownership. Fortunately, the majority of Westie breeders is devoted to the breed and its well-being. New owners should have little problem finding a reputable breeder who doesn't live in a different state or on the other side of the country. The American Kennel Club is able to refer you to breeders of quality West Highland White Terriers, as can any local

Although most breeders will not allow potential customers to visit the litter when it's this young, you should be able to visit the litter by around the fifth week or later.

working lines. The real quality breeders are quiet and unassuming. You hear about them at dog shows and other club events, by word of mouth. You may be well advised to avoid the novice who lives only a couple miles away. The local novice breeder, trying so hard to get rid of that first litter of puppies, is more than accommodating and anxious to sell you one. That breeder will charge you as much as an established breeder. The novice breeder isn't going to interrogate you and your family about your intentions with the puppy, the environment and training you can provide, etc. That breeder will be nowhere to be found when your poorly bred, badly adjusted four-pawed monster starts to growl and spit up at midnight or eat the family cat!

While the West Highland White Terrier is generally a hardy breed, socialization is a breeder

TIME TO GO HOME

Breeders rarely release puppies until they are eight to ten weeks of age. This is an acceptable age for most breeds of dog, excepting toy breeds, which are not released until around 12 weeks, given their petite sizes. If a breeder has a puppy that is 12 weeks or more, it is likely well socialized and house-trained. Be sure that it is otherwise healthy before deciding to take it home.

all-breed club or Westie club. Potential owners are encouraged to attend a dog show to meet the handlers firsthand and to get an idea what West Highland White Terriers look like outside a photographer's lens. Provided you approach the handlers when they are not terribly busy with the dogs, most are more than willing to answer questions, recommend breeders and give advice.

Now that you have contacted and met a breeder or two and made your choice about which breeder is best suited to your needs, it's time to visit the litter. Keep in mind that many top breeders have waiting lists. Sometimes new owners have to wait as long as two years for a puppy. If you are really committed to the breeder whom you've selected, then you will wait (and hope for an early arrival!). If not, you may have to resort to your second- or third-choice breeder. Don't be too anxious, however. If the breeder

doesn't have any waiting list, or any customers, there is probably a good reason. It's no different than visiting a café with no clientele. The better cafés and restaurants always have a waiting list—and it's usually worth the wait. Besides, isn't a puppy more important than a good meal?

Since you are likely choosing a West Highland White Terrier as a pet dog and not as a show dog, you simply should select a pup that is friendly and attractive. While the basic structure of the breed has little variation, the temperament may present trouble in certain strains. Beware of the shy or overly aggressive puppy; be especially conscious of the

At this Scottish-Irish festival, many native breeds are on display, and it is a good opportunity to meet dogs and their owners.

PET INSURANCE

Just like you can insure your car, your house and your own health, you likewise can insure your dog's health. Investigate a pet insurance policy by talking to your vet. Depending on the age of your dog, the breed and the kind of coverage you desire, your policy can be very affordable. Most policies cover accidental injuries, poisoning and thousands of medical problems and illnesses. Some carriers also cover routine care and immunization coverage, including spaying/neutering, health screening and more. These policies are more costly than the others, but may be well worth the investment.

Your breeder should be able to show you the dam's bite if you are concerned about the puppy's mouth. This adult possesses the desired scissors bite.

tenth week. Breeders who permit their puppies to leave early are more interested in your money than their puppies' well-being. Puppies need to learn the rules of the trade from their dams, and most dams continue teaching the pups manners and dos and don'ts until around the eighth week. Breeders spend significant amounts of time with the Westie toddlers so that they are able to interact with the "other species," i.e., humans. Given the long history that dogs and humans have, bonding between the two species is natural but must be nurtured. A well-bred, well-socialized West Highland White Terrier pup wants nothing more than to be near you and please you.

nervous West Highland White Terrier pup. Don't let sentiment or emotion trap you into buying the runt of the litter.

The gender of your puppy is largely a matter of personal taste, although there is a common belief among fanciers that bitches are quicker to learn and generally more loving and faithful. Males learn more slowly but retain the lesson longer. The difference in size is noticeable but slight.

Breeders commonly allow visitors to see the litter by around the fifth or sixth week, and puppies leave for their new homes between the eighth and

PERSONALITY PLUS

Your selection of a good puppy can be determined by your needs. A show potential or a good pet? It is your choice. Every puppy, however, should be of good temperament. Although show-quality puppies are bred and raised with emphasis on physical conformation, responsible breeders strive for equally good temperament. Do not buy from a breeder who concentrates solely on physical beauty at the expense of personality.

PEDIGREE VS. REGISTRATION CERTIFICATE

Your puppy's pedigree, essentially a family tree, is a written record of a dog's genealogy of three genera- tions or more. The pedigree will show you the names as well as performance titles of all dogs in your pup's background. Your breeder must provide you with a registration application, with his part properly filled out. You must complete the application and send it to the AKC with the proper fee. Every puppy must come from a litter that has been AKC-registered by the breeder, born in the U.S. and from a sire and dam that are also registered with the AKC.

The AKC requires that the seller provide the buyer with the following: breed; sex; color; date of birth; litter number (when available); names and registration numbers of the parents; breeder's name; and date sold or delivered.

Always check the bite of your selected puppy to be sure that it is neither overshot or undershot. This may not be too noticeable on a young puppy but it is important to check for overall soundness.

COMMITMENT OF OWNERSHIP

After considering all of these factors, you have most likely already made some very important decisions about selecting your puppy. You have chosen a West Highland White Terrier, which means that you have decided which characteris- tics you want in a dog and what type of dog will best fit into your family and lifestyle. If you have selected a breeder, you have gone a step further—you have done your research and found a respon- sible, conscientious person who breeds quality West Highland White Terriers and who should be a reliable source of help as you and your puppy adjust to life together. If you have observed a litter in action, you have obtained a firsthand look at the dynamics of a puppy "pack" and, thus, you

You should be so lucky as to have a litter as frisky and alert as this one from which to choose your new Westie! Select the puppy with the personality and energy that appeals to you.

temperament. You will be able to pick out which pups are the leaders, which ones are less outgoing, which ones are confident, which ones are shy, playful, friendly, aggressive, etc. Equally as important, you will learn to recognize what a healthy pup should look and act like. All of these things will help you in your search, and when you find the West Highland White Terrier that was meant for you, you will know it!

Researching your breed, selecting a responsible breeder and observing as many pups as possible are all important steps on the way to dog ownership. It may seem like a lot of effort...and you have not even brought the pup home yet! Remember, though, you cannot be too careful when it comes to deciding on the type of

Your new Westie will make himself at home in no time. Provide all the comforts of home, including security and affection.

should learn about each pup's individual personality—perhaps you have even found one that particularly appeals to you.

However, even if you have not yet found the West Highland White Terrier puppy of your dreams, observing pups will help you learn to recognize certain behavior and to determine what a pup's behavior indicates about his

YOUR SCHEDULE

If you lead an erratic, unpredictable life, with daily or weekly changes in your work requirements, consider the problems of owning a puppy. The new puppy has to be fed regularly, socialized (loved, petted, handled, introduced to other people) and, most importantly, allowed to visit outdoors for house-training. As the dog gets older, it can be more tolerant of deviations in its feeding and house-training relief.

dog you want and finding out about your prospective pup's background. Buying a puppy is not—or *should* not be—just another whimsical purchase. This is one instance in which you actually do get to choose your own family! You may be thinking that buying a puppy should be fun—it should not be so serious and so much work. Keep in mind that your puppy is not a cuddly stuffed toy or decorative lawn ornament, but a creature that will become a real member of your family. You will come to realize that, while buying a puppy is a

READY, SET, GO!
Unfortunately, when a puppy is bought by someone who does not take into consideration the time and attention that dog ownership requires, it is the puppy who suffers when he is either abandoned or placed in a shelter by a frustrated owner. So all of the "homework" you do in preparation for your pup's arrival will benefit you both. The more informed you are, the more you will know what to expect and the better equipped you will be to handle the ups and downs of raising a puppy. Hopefully, everyone in the household is willing to do his part in raising and caring for the pup. The anticipation of owning a dog often brings a lot of promises from excited family members: "I will walk him every day," "I will feed him," "I will housebreak him," etc., but these things take time and effort, and promises can easily be forgotten once the novelty of the new pet has worn off.

As anxious and curious as your Westie puppy is, do not let him run unattended through your yard. A puppy is virtually helpless in the human world and relies upon you for protection.

pleasurable and exciting endeavor, it is not something to be taken lightly. Relax…the fun will start when the pup comes home!

Always keep in mind that a puppy is nothing more than a baby in a furry disguise…a baby who is virtually helpless in a human world and who trusts his owner for fulfillment of his basic needs for survival. In addition to food, water and shelter, your pup needs care, protection, guidance and love. If you are not prepared to commit to this, then you are not prepared to own a dog.

"Wait a minute," you say. "How hard could this be? All of my neighbors own dogs and they seem to be doing just fine. Why should I have to worry about all of this?" Well, you should not worry about it; in fact, you will probably find that once your West Highland White Terrier pup gets used to his new home, he will fall into his place in the family quite naturally. But it never hurts to emphasize the commitment of dog ownership. With some time and patience, it is really not too difficult to raise a curious and exuberant West Highland White Terrier pup to become a well-

adjusted and well-mannered adult dog—a dog that could be your most loyal friend.

PREPARING PUPPY'S PLACE IN YOUR HOME

Researching your breed and finding a breeder are only two aspects of the "homework" you will have to do before bringing your West Highland White Terrier puppy home. You will also have to prepare your home and family for the new addition. Much like you would prepare a nursery for a newborn baby, you will need to designate a place in your home that will be the puppy's own. How you prepare your home will depend on how much freedom the dog will be allowed. Will he be confined to one room or a specific area in the house, or will he be allowed to roam as he pleases? Will he spend most of his time in the house or will he be primarily an outdoor dog? Whatever you decide, you must ensure that he has a place that he can "call his own."

When you bring your new puppy into your home, you are bringing him into what will become his home as well. Obviously, you did not buy a puppy so that he could take over your house, but in order for a puppy to grow into a stable, well-adjusted dog, he has to feel comfortable in his surroundings. Remember, he is leaving the warmth and security of his

FOLLOW THE BREEDER'S LEAD
You will probably start feeding your pup the same food that he has been getting from the breeder; the breeder should give you a few days' supply to start you off. Although you should not give your pup too many treats, you will want to have puppy treats on hand for coaxing, training, rewards, etc. Be careful, though, as a small pup's calorie requirements are relatively low and a few treats can add up to almost a full day's worth of calories without the required nutrition.

mother and littermates, as well as the familiarity of the only place he has ever known, so it is important to make his transition as easy as possible. By preparing a place in your home for the puppy, you are making him feel as welcome as possible in a strange new place. It should not take him long to get used to it, but the sudden shock of being transplanted is somewhat traumatic for a young pup. Imagine how a small child would feel in the same situation—that is how your puppy must be feeling.

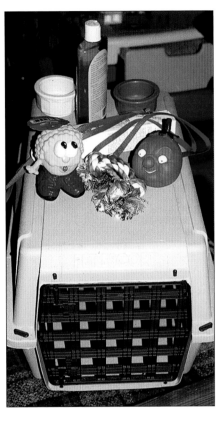

Be prepared for your pup's arrival. Ask your breeder to recommend the equipment you will need.

It is up to you to reassure him and to let him know, "Little fellow, you are going to like it here!"

WHAT YOU SHOULD BUY
CRATE
To someone unfamiliar with the use of crates in dog training, it may seem like punishment to shut a dog in a crate, but this is not the case at all. Crates are not cruel—crates have many humane and highly effective uses in dog care and training. For example,

---

A CLEAN DEN

During crate training, you should partition off the section of the crate in which the pup stays. If he is given too big an area, this will hinder your training efforts. Crate training is based on the fact that a dog does not like to soil his sleeping quarters, so it is ineffective to keep a pup in an area that is so big that he can eliminate in one end and get far enough away from it to sleep. Also, you want to make the crate den-like for the pup. Blankets and a favorite toy will make the crate cozy for the small pup. As he grows, you should remove the partition to give him access to the entire crate.

It will take some coaxing at first, but given some time, your pup will adapt to his new home-within-a-home quite nicely.

PHOTO COURTESY OF DOSKOCIL.

Terrier can curl up in his crate when he wants to sleep or when he just needs a break. Many dogs sleep in their crates overnight. With a nice crate pad and a favorite toy, a crate becomes a cozy pseudo-den for your dog. Like his ancestors, he too will seek out the comfort and retreat of a den—you just happen to be providing him with something a little more luxurious than leaves and twigs lining a dirty ditch.

As far as purchasing a crate, the type that you buy is up to you. It will most likely be one of the two most popular types: wire or fiberglass. There are advantages and disadvantages to each type. For example, a wire crate is more open, allowing the air to flow through and affording the dog a view of what is going on around him. A fiberglass crate, however, is sturdier and can double as a travel crate since it provides more protection for the dog. The size of the crate is another thing to consider. Puppies do not stay puppies forever—in fact, sometimes it seems as if they grow right before your eyes. A Yorkie-sized crate may be fine for a very young West Highland White Terrier pup, but it will not do him much good for long! Unless you have the money and the inclination to buy a new crate every time your pup has a growth spurt, it is better to get one that will

Your local pet shop can offer many types and sizes of crates. These are three standard fiberglass crates.

crate training is a very popular and very successful house-breaking method. A crate can keep your dog safe during travel and, perhaps most importantly, a crate provides your dog with a place of his own in your home. It serves as a "doggie bedroom" of sorts—your West Highland White accommodate your dog both as a pup and at full size.

BEDDING

A soft crate pad in the dog's crate will help the dog feel more at home and you may toss in a small blanket. First, the bedding will take the place of the leaves, twigs, etc., that the pup would use in the wild to make a den; the pup can make his own "burrow" in the crate. Although your pup is far removed from his den-making ancestors, the

Westies love to have a bed of their own with a soft blanket. The bedding should be washed frequently as the dog may soil it with his feet.

THE PUP'S TOY BOX

With a big variety of dog toys available, and so many that look like they would be a lot of fun for a dog, be careful in your selection. It is amazing what a set of puppy teeth can do to an innocent-looking toy, so, obviously, safety is a major consideration. Be sure to choose the most durable products that you can find. Hard nylon bones and toys are a safe bet, and many of them are offered in different scents and flavors that will be sure to capture your dog's attention. It is always fun to play a game of catch with your dog, and there are balls and flying discs that are specially made to withstand dog teeth.

denning instinct is still a part of his genetic makeup. Second, until you bring your pup home, he has been sleeping amid the warmth of his mother and litter-mates, and while a blanket is not the same as a warm, breathing body, it still provides heat and something with which to snuggle. You will want to wash your pup's blankets frequently in case he has an accident in his crate, and replace or remove any blanket that becomes ragged and starts to fall apart.

TOYS

Toys are a must for dogs of all ages, especially for curious, playful pups. Puppies are the "children" of the dog world, and what child does not love toys? Chew toys provide enjoyment to

You will need different kinds of dog toys for chewing, exercise and entertainment. Be careful! Poorly made toys can be very dangerous as Westies can easily chew them apart and swallow the pieces.

PHOTO COURTESY OF MIKKI PET PRODUCTS.

THE COSTS OF OWNERSHIP

Grooming tools, collars, leashes, dog beds and, of course, toys will be expenses to you when you first obtain your pup, and the cost will trickle on throughout your dog's lifetime. If your puppy damages or destroys your possessions (as most puppies surely will!) or something belonging to a neighbor, you can calculate additional expense. There is also flea and pest control, which every dog owner faces more than once. You must be able to handle the financial responsibility of owning a dog.

both dog and owner—your dog will enjoy playing with his favorite toys, while you will enjoy the fact that they distract him from your expensive shoes and leather sofa. Puppies love to chew; in fact, chewing is a physical need for pups as they are teething, and everything looks appetizing! The full range of your possessions—from old dishrag to Oriental rug—are fair game in the eyes of a teething pup. Puppies are not all that discerning when it comes to finding something to literally "sink their teeth into"—

everything tastes great!

West Highland White Terrier puppies are fairly aggressive chewers, as is true of most of the terrier breeds. Breeders advise owners to resist stuffed toys because they can become de-stuffed in no time. The overly excited pup may ingest the stuffing, which is neither nutritious nor digestible.

Similarly, squeaky toys are quite popular, but should be avoided for the West Highland White Terrier. Perhaps a squeaky toy can be used as an aid in training, but not for free play. If a pup "disembowels" one of these, the small plastic squeaker inside can be dangerous if swallowed. Monitor the condition of all your pup's toys carefully and get rid of any that have been chewed to

Your local pet shop usually carries a very complete selection of leashes.

the point of becoming potentially dangerous.

Be careful of natural bones, which have a tendency to splinter into sharp, dangerous pieces. Also be careful of rawhide, which can turn into pieces that are easy to swallow or into a mushy mess on your carpet.

Westie puppies must chew. Soft toys, besides being expensive and easily destroyed, can be dangerous should the puppy swallow bits and pieces.

LEASH

A nylon leash is probably the best option as it is the most resistant to puppy teeth should your pup take a liking to chewing on his leash. Of course, this is a habit that should be nipped in the bud, but if your pup likes to chew on his leash, he has a very slim chance of being able to chew through the strong nylon. Nylon leashes are also lightweight, which is good for a young West Highland White Terrier who is just getting used to the idea of walking on a leash. For everyday walking and safety purposes, the nylon leash is a good choice. As your pup grows up and gets used to walking on the leash, you may want to purchase a flexible leash. These leashes allow you to extend the length to give the dog a broader area to explore or to shorten the length to keep the dog close to you.

Collar

Your pup should get used to wearing a collar all the time since you will want to attach his ID tags to it. Plus, you have to attach the

Westies will enjoy rawhide chews, but only offer them under supervision.

leash to something! A lightweight nylon collar is a good choice; make sure that it fits snugly enough so that the pup cannot wriggle out of it, but is loose enough so that it will not be uncomfortably tight around the pup's neck. You should be able to fit a finger between the pup and the collar. It may take some time for your pup to get used to wearing the collar, but soon he will not even notice that it is there. Choke collars are made for training, but should only be used by an experienced handler.

Food and Water Bowls

Your pup will need two bowls, one for food and one for water. You may want two sets of bowls, one for inside and one for outside, depending on where the dog will be fed and where he will be spending time. Stainless steel or sturdy plastic bowls are popular choices. Plastic bowls are more chewable. Dogs tend not to chew on the steel variety, which can be sterilized. It is important to buy sturdy bowls since anything is in danger of being chewed by puppy teeth and you do not want your dog to be constantly chewing apart his bowl (for his safety and for your purse!).

Cleaning Supplies

Until a pup is house-trained, you will be doing a lot of cleaning. "Accidents" will occur, which is okay in the beginning because the puppy does not know any better. All you can do is be prepared to clean up any accidents. Old rags, towels, newspapers and a safe disinfectant are good to have on hand.

BEYOND THE BASICS

The items previously discussed are the bare necessities. You will find out what else you need as you go along—grooming supplies, flea/tick protection, baby gates to partition a room, etc. These things will vary depending on your situation but it is important that you have everything you need to feed and make your West Highland White Terrier comfortable in his first few days at home.

Your local pet shop should have a variety of food and water bowls, or combinations thereof, made from metal, plastic and crockery.

Never fail to clean up your dog's waste, even if in your own yard. Your pet shop has accessories to assist you in this necessary task.

PHOTO COURTESY OF MIKKI PET PRODUCTS.

Westie puppies are very inquisitive. Your yard should be free of plants that are toxic or contain herbicides, which can be poisonous. Flowers also attract wasps and bees, both of which attack dogs when provoked.

PUPPY-PROOFING YOUR HOME

Aside from making sure that your West Highland White Terrier will be comfortable in your home, you also have to make sure that your home is safe for your West Highland White Terrier. This means taking precautions that your pup will not get into anything he should not get into and that there is nothing within his reach that may harm him should he sniff it, chew it, inspect it, etc. This probably seems obvious since, while you are primarily concerned with your pup's safety, at the same time you do not want your belongings to be ruined. Breakables should be placed out of reach if your dog is to have full run of the house. If he is to be limited to certain places within the house, keep any potentially dangerous items in the "off-limits" areas. An electrical

cord can pose a danger should the puppy decide to taste it—and who is going to convince a pup that it would not make a great chew toy? Cords should be fastened tightly against the wall. If your dog is going to spend time in a crate, make sure that there is nothing near his crate that he can reach if he sticks his curious little nose or paws through the openings. Just as you would with a child, keep all household cleaners and chemicals where the pup cannot get to them.

It is also important to make sure that the outside of your home is safe. Of course your puppy should never be unsupervised, but a pup let loose in the yard will want to run and explore, and he

---

GARDEN OF DOOM

Many plants can be toxic to dogs. If you see your dog carrying a piece of vegetation in his mouth, approach him in a quiet, disinterested manner, avoid eye contact, pet him and gradually remove the plant from his mouth. Alternatively, offer him a treat and maybe he'll drop the plant on his own accord. Be sure no toxic plants are growing in your own garden.

jump or climb over a fence. The remedy is to make the fence high enough so that it really is impossible for your dog to get over it (about 6 feet should suffice), and well embedded into the ground. Be sure to repair or secure any gaps in the fence. Check the fence periodically to ensure that it is in good shape and make repairs as needed; a very determined pup may return to the same spot to "work on it" until he is able to get through. This is especially true with a terrier like your Westie.

Your Westie's first visit to the vet will be an overall examination. Take your new dog to your veterinarian as soon as possible.

should be granted that freedom. Do not let a fence give you a false sense of security; you would be surprised how crafty (and persistent) a dog can be in figuring out how to dig under and squeeze his way through small holes, or to

SKULL & CROSSBONES
Thoroughly puppy-proof your house before bringing your puppy home. Never use roach or rodent poisons in any area accessible to the puppy. Avoid the use of toilet-bowl cleaners. Most dogs are born with toilet-bowl sonar and will take a drink if the lid is left open. Also keep the trash secured and out of reach.

FIRST TRIP TO THE VET
You have picked out your puppy, and your home and family are ready. Now all you have to do is collect your West Highland White Terrier from the breeder and the fun begins, right? Well...not so fast. Something else you need to schedule is your pup's first trip to the veterinarian. Perhaps the breeder can recommend someone in the area who specializes in West Highland White Terriers, or

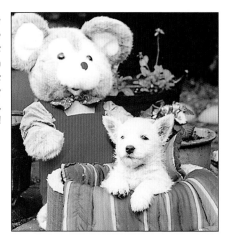

Make your Westie feel welcome to your home, but don't overwhelm him in the first day. He's already had a long, rough day!

maybe you know some other Westie owners who can suggest a good vet. Either way, you should have an appointment arranged for your pup before you pick him up and plan on taking him for an examination before bringing him home.

The pup's first visit will consist of an overall examination to make sure that the pup does not have any problems that are not apparent to you. The veterinarian will also set up a schedule for the pup's vaccinations; the breeder will inform you of which ones the pup has already received and the vet can continue from there.

INTRODUCTION TO THE FAMILY

Everyone in the house will be excited about the puppy's coming home and will want to pet him and play with him, but it is best to make the introduction low-key so as not to overwhelm the puppy. He is apprehensive already. It is the first time he has been separated from his mother and the breeder, and the ride to your home is likely the first time he has been in a car. The last thing you want to do is smother him, as this will only frighten him further. This is not to say that human contact is not extremely necessary at this stage because this is the time when a connection between the pup and his human family is formed. Gentle petting and soothing words should help console him, as well as just putting him down and letting him explore on his own under your watchful eye.

The pup may approach the family members or may busy himself with exploring for a while. Gradually, each person should spend some time with the

HOUSEHOLD DANGERS

Scour your garage for potential puppy dangers. Remove weed killers, rose fertilizers, pesticides and antifreeze materials. Antifreeze is highly toxic and just a few drops can kill a puppy or adult dog. The sweet taste attracts the animal, who will quickly consume it from the floor or curbside.

pup, one at a time, crouching down to get as close to the pup's level as possible and letting him sniff their hands and petting him gently. He definitely needs human attention and he needs to be touched—this is how to form an immediate bond. Just remember that the pup is experiencing a lot of things for the first time, at the same time. There are new people, new noises, new smells and new things to investigate so be gentle, be affectionate and be as comforting as you can.

YOUR PUP'S FIRST NIGHT HOME

You have traveled home with your new charge safely in his crate. He's been to the vet for a thorough check-up; he's been weighed, his papers examined; perhaps he's even been vaccinated and wormed as well. He's met the family, licked the whole family, including the excited children and the less-than-happy cat. He's explored his area, his new bed, the yard and anywhere else he's been permitted. He's eaten his first meal at home and relieved himself in the proper place. He's heard lots of new sounds, smelled new friends and seen more of the outside world than ever before.

That was just the first day! He's tuckered out and is ready for bed...or so you think!

It's puppy's first night and you are ready to say "Good night"— keep in mind that this is puppy's first night ever to be sleeping alone. His dam and littermates are no longer at paw's length and he's a bit scared, cold and lonely. Be reassuring to your new family member. This is not the time to spoil him and give in to his inevitable whining.

Puppies whine. They whine to let the others know where they are and hopefully to get company out of it. Place your pup in his new bed or crate in his room and close the door. Mercifully, he may fall asleep without a peep. When the inevitable occurs, ignore the whining; he is fine. Be strong and keep his interest in mind. Do not allow your heart to become guilty and visit the pup. He will fall asleep.

Many breeders recommend placing a piece of bedding from his former home in his new bed so that he recognizes the scent of his littermates. Others still advise placing a hot water bottle in his bed for warmth. The latter may be

Your new Westie puppy must be under constant supervision. He might find himself in a dangerous situation, especially if he tries to explore the grounds by himself.

a good idea provided the pup doesn't attempt to suckle—he'll get good and wet and may not fall asleep so fast.

Puppy's first night can be somewhat stressful for the pup and his new family. Remember that you are setting the tone of nighttime at your house. Unless you want to play with your pup every night at 10 p.m., midnight and 2 a.m., don't initiate the habit. Your family will thank you, and so will your pup!

PREVENTING PUPPY PROBLEMS
SOCIALIZATION

Now that you have done all of the preparatory work and have helped your pup get accustomed to his new home and family, it is about time for you to have some fun! Socializing your West Highland White Terrier pup gives you the opportunity to show off your new

HAPPY TO MEET YOU

Thorough socialization includes not only meeting new people but also being introduced to new experiences such as riding in the car, having his coat brushed, hearing the television, walking in a crowd—the list is endless. The more your pup experiences, and the more positive the experiences are, the less of a shock and the less scary it will be for your pup to encounter new things.

friend, and your pup gets to reap the benefits of being an adorable furry creature that people want to pet and, in general, think is absolutely precious!

Besides getting to know his new family, your puppy should be exposed to other people, animals and situations. This will help him become well adjusted as he grows up and less prone to being timid or fearful of the new things he will encounter. Your pup's socialization began at the breeder's but now it is your responsibility to continue it. The socialization he receives up until the age of 12 weeks is the most critical, as this is the time when he forms his impressions of the outside world. Be especially careful during the eight-to-ten-week-old period, also known as the fear period. The interaction he receives during this time should be gentle and reassuring. Lack of socialization can manifest itself in fear and aggression as the dog grows up. He needs lots of human contact, affection, handling and exposure to other animals.

Once your pup has received his necessary vaccinations, feel free to take him out and about (on his leash, of course). Walk him around the neighborhood, take him on your daily errands, let people pet him, let him meet other dogs and pets, etc. Puppies do not have to try to make friends; there will be no shortage of people who will want to introduce themselves. Just make sure that you carefully supervise each meeting. If the neighborhood children want to say hello, for example, that is great—children and pups most often make great companions. However, sometimes an excited child can unintentionally handle a pup too roughly, or an overzealous pup can playfully nip a little too hard. You want to make socialization experiences positive ones. What a pup learns during this very formative stage will impact his attitude toward future encounters. You want your dog to be comfortable around everyone. A pup that has a bad experience with a child may grow up to be a dog that is shy around or aggressive toward children.

Socialization is important. Your new Westie should meet his human friends as well as his canine associates.

CONSISTENCY IN TRAINING

Dogs, being pack animals, naturally need a leader, or else they try to establish dominance in their packs. When you bring a dog into your

family, the choice of who becomes the leader and who becomes the "pack" is entirely up to you! Your pup's intuitive quest for dominance, coupled with the fact that it is nearly impossible to look at an adorable West Highland White Terrier pup, with his "puppy-dog" eyes and black button nose, and not cave in, give the pup almost an unfair advantage in getting the upper hand! A pup will definitely test the waters to see what he can and cannot do. Do not give in to those dark pleading eyes—stand your ground when it comes to

IN DUE TIME

It will take at least two weeks for your puppy to become accustomed to his new surroundings. Give him lots of love, attention, handling, frequent opportunities to relieve himself, a diet he likes to eat and a place he can call his own.

Early training pays you dividends for the life of your dog. The Westie's personality is shaped by early training.

disciplining the pup and make sure that all family members do the same. It will only confuse the pup when Mother tells him to get off the couch when he is used to sitting up there with Father to watch the nightly news. Avoid discrepancies by having all members of the household decide on the rules before the pup even comes home…and be consistent in enforcing them! Early training shapes the dog's personality, so you cannot be unclear in what you expect.

COMMON PUPPY PROBLEMS

The best way to prevent puppy problems is to be proactive in stopping an undesirable behavior as soon as it starts. The old saying "You can't teach an old dog new tricks" does not necessarily hold

true, but it is true that it is much easier to discourage bad behavior in a young developing pup than to wait until the pup's bad behavior becomes the adult dog's bad habit. There are some problems that are especially prevalent in puppies as they develop.

NIPPING

As puppies start to teethe, they feel the need to sink their teeth into anything available…unfortunately that includes your fingers, arms, hair and toes. You may find this behavior cute for the first five seconds…until you feel just how sharp those puppy teeth are. This is something you want to discourage immediately and consistently with a firm "No!" (or whatever number of firm "Nos" it takes for him to understand that you mean business). Then replace your finger with an appropriate chew toy. While this behavior is merely annoying when the dog is young, it can become dangerous as your West Highland White Terrier's adult teeth grow in and his jaws develop, and he continues to think it is okay to gnaw on human appendages. Your Westie does not mean any harm with a friendly nip, but he also does not know the strength of his large terrier teeth.

CRYING/WHINING

Your pup will often cry, whine, whimper, howl or make some

type of commotion when he is left alone. This is basically his way of calling out for attention to make sure that you know he is there and that you have not forgotten about him. He feels insecure when he is left alone, when you are out of the house and he is in his crate or when you are in another part of the house and he cannot see you. The noise he is making is an expression of the anxiety he feels at being alone, so he needs to be taught that being alone is okay. You are not actually training the dog to stop making noise, you are training him to feel comfortable when he is alone and thus removing the need for him to make the noise. This is where the crate with a toy and a cozy blanket comes in handy. You want to know that he is safe when you are not there to supervise, and you know that he will be safe in his crate rather than roaming freely about the house. In order for the pup to stay in his crate without making a fuss, he needs to be comfortable in his crate. On that note, it is extremely important that the crate is never used as a form of punishment, or the pup will develop a negative association with the crate.

Accustom the pup to the crate in short, gradually increasing time intervals in which you put him in the crate, maybe with a treat, and stay in the room with him. If he cries or makes a fuss, do not go to him, but stay in his sight. Gradually he will realize that staying in his crate is all right without your help, and it will not be so traumatic for him when you are not around. You may want to leave the radio on softly when you leave the house; the sound of human voices may be comforting to him.

THOSE GROWING TERRIER TEETH

Chewing goes hand in hand with nipping in the sense that a teething puppy is always looking for a way to soothe his aching gums. In this case, instead of chewing on you, he may have taken a liking to your favorite shoe or something else which he should not be chewing. Again, realize that this is a normal canine behavior that does not need to be discouraged, only redirected. Your pup just needs to be taught what is acceptable to chew on and what is off-limits. Consistently tell him "No" when you catch him chewing on something forbidden and give him a chew toy. Conversely, praise him when you catch him chewing on something appropriate. In this way you are discouraging the inappropriate behavior and reinforcing the desired behavior. The puppy's chewing should stop after his adult teeth have come in, but an adult dog continues to chew for various reasons—perhaps because he is bored, needs to relieve tension or just likes to chew. That is why it is important to redirect his chewing when he is still young.

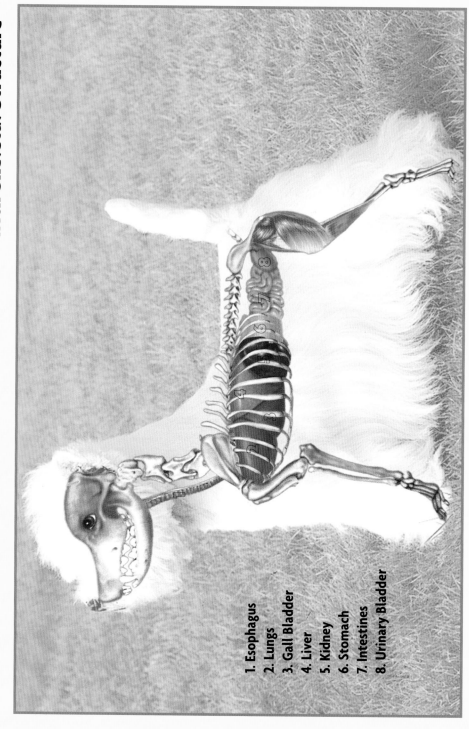

1. Esophagus
2. Lungs
3. Gall Bladder
4. Liver
5. Kidney
6. Stomach
7. Intestines
8. Urinary Bladder

WEST HIGHLAND WHITE TERRIER

DIETARY AND FEEDING CONSIDERATIONS

You have probably heard it a thousand times, "You are what you eat." Believe it or not, it's very true. Dogs are what you feed them because they have little choice in the matter. Even those people who truly want to feed their dogs the best often cannot do so because they do not know which foods are best for their dogs.

Dog foods are produced in three basic types: dry, semi-moist and canned. Dry foods are the choice of the cost-conscious because they are much less expensive than semi-moist and canned. Dry foods contain the least fat and the most preserva-

FOOD PREFERENCE

Selecting the best dried dog food is difficult. There is no majority consensus among veterinary scientists as to the value of nutrient analyses (protein, fat, fiber, moisture, ash, cholesterol, minerals, etc.). All agree that feeding trials are what matter, but you also have to consider the individual dog. Its weight, age, activity and what pleases its taste all must be considered. It is probably best to take the advice of your veterinarian. Every dog's dietary requirements vary, even during the lifetime of a particular dog.

If your dog is fed a good dry food, it does not require supplements of meat or vegetables. Dogs do appreciate a little variety in their diets so you may choose to stay with the same brand, but vary the flavor. Alternatively, you may wish to add a little flavored stock to alter or enhance the taste.

You cannot have a happy, healthy Westie if you offer him a poor diet. A balanced dog food and plenty of water are essential; follow the advice of your breeder.

tives. Most canned foods are 60–70-percent water, while semi-moist foods are so full of sugar that they are the least preferred by owners, though

Newborn puppies should begin suckling almost immediately. If they fail to suckle when placed onto their mother's teats, they must be hand-fed on a special formula.

dogs welcome them (as a child does candy).

Three stages of development must be considered when selecting

FEEDING TIPS

- Dog food must be served at room temperature, neither too hot nor too cold. Fresh water, changed often and served in a clean bowl, is mandatory, especially when feeding dry food.
- Never feed your dog from the table while you are eating, and never feed your dog leftovers from your own meal. They usually contain too much fat and too much seasoning.
- Dogs must chew their food. Hard pellets are excellent; soups and stews are to be avoided.
- Don't add leftovers or any extras to commercial dog food. The normal food is usually balanced, and adding something extra destroys the balance.
- Except for age-related changes, dogs do not require dietary variations. They can be fed the same diet, day after day, without their becoming bored or ill.

At six weeks of age, puppies are introduced to canned meat. Most Westie pups wean from the dam with no problems.

a diet for your dog: the puppy stage, the mid-age or adult stage and the senior stage.

PUPPY STAGE

Puppies have a natural instinct to suck milk from their mother's teats. They exhibit this behavior from the first moments of their lives. If they don't suckle within a short while, the breeder attempts to put them onto their mother's nipples. A newborn's failure to suckle often requires that the breeder hand-feed the pup under the guidance of a veterinarian. This involves a baby bottle and a special formula. Their mother's milk is much better than any formula because it contains colostrum, a sort of antibiotic milk that protects the puppies during the first eight to ten weeks of their lives.

Puppies should be allowed to nurse for six weeks, and then they should be slowly weaned away from their mother by introducing

TEST FOR PROPER DIET
A good test for proper diet is the color, odor and firmness of your dog's stool. A healthy dog usually produces three semi-hard stools per day. The stools should have no unpleasant odor. They should be the same color from excretion to excretion.

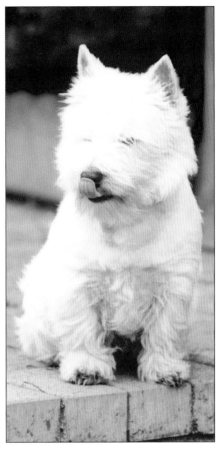

Hurray for tasty victuals! Westies are usually hearty eaters that do not need much encouragement at dinner time.

small portions of canned meat after they are about one month old. Dry food is then gradually added to the puppies' portions over the next few weeks.

By the time they are eight weeks old, they should be completely weaned and fed solely a puppy dry food. During this period, the selection of diet is most important as the puppy grows fastest during its first year of life.

West Highland White Terrier pups should be fed three meals per

day when they are six to eight weeks of age. At eight weeks, the pup can be fed twice per day. Fussy eaters may require an additional smaller meal to maintain a good weight. Growth foods can be recommended by your veterinarian and the puppy should be kept on this diet for up to 18 months.

Puppy diets should be balanced for your dog's needs,

Food treats can be used as motivators in training or rewards for a job well done, but be careful not to give your Westie too many treats.

and supplements of vitamins, minerals and protein should not be necessary.

ADULT DIETS

A dog is considered an adult when it has stopped growing in height and/or length. Do not consider the dog's weight when the decision is made to switch from a puppy diet to a maintenance diet. Again you should rely upon your veterinarian to recommend an acceptable adult maintenance diet. Major dog food manufacturers specialize in this type of food and it is only necessary for you to select the one best suited to your dog's needs. Active dogs may have different requirements than sedate dogs.

A West Highland White Terrier is fully mature around 12 months of age, though it often takes another 12 to 18 months for the dog to reach its peak as a performance animal.

SENIOR DIETS

As dogs get older, their metabolism changes. The older dog usually exercises less, moves more slowly and sleeps more. This change in lifestyle and physiological performance requires a change in diet. Since these changes take place slowly, they might not be recognizable. What is easily recognizable is weight gain. By continually feeding your dog an adult

> **As your Westie grows, his nutritional needs will change. Your vet can help you plan a proper feeding schedule for your dog.**

> **FOOD STORAGE**
> You must store your dry dog food carefully. Open packages of dog food quickly lose their vitamin value, usually within 90 days of being opened. Mold spores and vermin could also contaminate the food.

maintenance diet when it is slowing down metabolically, your dog will gain weight. Obesity in an older dog compounds the health problems that may accompany old age.

As dogs get older, few of their organs function up to par. The kidneys slow down and the intestines become less efficient. These age-related factors are best handled with a change in diet and a change in feeding schedule to give smaller portions that are more easily digested.

There is no single best diet for every older dog. While many dogs do well on light or senior diets, other dogs do better on puppy diets or other special premium diets such as lamb and rice.

Be sensitive to your senior West Highland White Terrier's diet, and this will help control other problems that may arise with your old friend.

Westies do not need organized trials to get proper exercise, but trained Westies thrive on the challenge and activity.

WATER
Just as your dog needs proper nutrition from his food, water is an essential "nutrient" as well. Water keeps the dog's body properly hydrated and promotes normal function of the body's systems. During housebreaking, it is necessary to keep an eye on how much water your West Highland White Terrier is drinking, but once he is reliably trained he should have access to clean fresh water at all times. Make sure that the dog's water bowl is clean and change the water often.

EXERCISE
All dogs require some form of exercise, regardless of breed. A sedentary lifestyle is as harmful to a dog as it is to a person. The West Highland White Terrier happens to be an above-average active breed that requires more exercise than most breeds. Regular walks, play sessions in the yard and letting the dog run free in the garden under your supervision are

Some dogs can be a bit sloppy about their feeding and drinking habits. This large cat pan solved the messy-floor problem easily.

GRAIN-BASED DIETS
Some less expensive dog foods are based on grains and other plant proteins. While these products may appear to be attractively priced, many breeders prefer a diet based on animal proteins and believe that they are more conducive to your dog's health. Many grain-based diets rely on soy protein, which may cause flatulence (passing gas).

There are many cases, however, when your dog might require a special diet. These special requirements should only be recommended by your veterinarian.

Whether pet dog or show dog, all Westies need regular grooming for healthy coats and skin.

all sufficient forms of exercise for the West Highland White Terrier. For those who are more ambitious, you will find that your West Highland White Terrier will be able to keep up with you on extra-long walks or your morning jog. Not only is exercise essential to keep the dog's body fit, it is essential to his mental well-being. A bored dog will find something to do, which often manifests itself in some type of destructive behavior. In this sense, it is essential for the owner's mental well-being as well!

GROOMING

Do understand before purchasing your Westie that this is a breed with a coat that needs mainte-nance, whether you have a dog for

the show ring or one that is a household pet. Think of it in terms of your child—you bathe your youngster, comb his hair and put a clean set of clothes on him. The end product is that you have a child who smells good, who looks nice and whom you enjoy having in your company. It is the same with your dog—keep the dog brushed, cleaned and trimmed, and you will find it a pleasure to be in his company. However, it will require some effort to do this.

The Westie is a double-coated dog. There is a dense, thick undercoat that protects the dog in all kinds of weather and there is a harsh outercoat. Coat care for the pet Westie can be much different and easier than the coat care for a

GROOMING OF YORE
A well-known early Westie breeder, Holland Buckley wrote in 1913: "Most people wash their dogs regularly. Unless preparing a puppy for a special purpose, do not bathe him at all, at least not artificially, but get him used to swimming in a pond or the river, never forgetting to give him a good gallop and a rub down afterwards. A few minutes spent each day with a comb and a dandy brush will keep the coat in tip-top condition, and the skin supple and healthy."

show dog. The vast majority of Westie fanciers have pet dogs and they should not expect to maintain show coats.

If you are planning to show your West Highland White Terrier, you will be ahead of the game if you purchase your puppy from a reputable breeder who grooms and shows his own dogs. If so, this is the individual to see for grooming lessons to learn how to get your dog ready for the show ring. Grooming for show is an art, and an art that cannot be learned in a few months. Furthermore, it is very difficult, but not impossible, to learn it from a book.

The primary difference between the pet and show Westie coat is that the show Westie will have a dense undercoat and on top of it he will have a shiny, harsh coat that will fit him like a jacket. With the proper coat, the dog presents a smartness in the ring that can be hard to beat. This coat can only be acquired by stripping the body coat with a stripping knife or stripping by hand. Within 10 to 12 weeks, and with the proper upkeep, he will have grown from his "underwear" outfit stage into a smart new outfit ready for the ring. This all takes skill, time and interest in order to do it well.

Pet grooming is different from grooming for the show ring as you use a clipper on the body and scissors for trimming the furnish-

ings. You will not have the harsh, tight-fitting jacket of the show Westie, but you will have a neat, clean and trimmed dog that will still look like a West Highland White Terrier. Even those with kennels who are active in the show ring will clip their old dogs or those who are no longer being shown.

Westies are great showmen. The Westie show coat is more dramatic than the pet clip, requiring many hours of stripping and preening.

A pin brush is used to groom the top of the head.

Grooming tools needed for the show Westie.

Chalk is used to "whiten" the Westie's coat. Professionals never get caught with dust on them!

Westies require meticulous grooming for the show ring. The Westie show coat is plucked by hand to get the desired rough appearance.

Here are the tools that you will need if you are going to do your own grooming:

1. A grooming table, something sturdy with a rubber mat covering the top. You will need a grooming arm, or a "hanger." (You can use a table in your laundry room with

an eye hook in the ceiling for holding the leash.) Your dog will now be comfortable even if confined and you will be able to work on the dog. Grooming is a very difficult and frustrating job if you try to groom without a table and a grooming arm.

2. A metal comb, a slicker brush, a good, sharp pair of scissors and a toenail trimmer.

3. Electric clippers with a #10 blade.

To start: Set your dog on the table and put the leash around his neck. Have your leash up behind the ears and have the leash taut when you fasten it to your eye hook. Do not walk away and leave your dog unattended as he can jump off the table and be left dangling from the leash with his feet scrambling around in the air.

Take your slicker brush and brush out the entire coat. Brush the whiskers toward the nose, the body hair toward the tail, the tail up toward the tip of the tail. Brush the leg furnishings up toward the body and brush the chest hair down toward the table. Hold the dog up by the front legs and gently brush the stomach hair, first

A scissors is used to trim the anal region to keep it clean and neat.

A metal comb is used to groom the trunk.

toward the head and then back toward the rear. For cleanliness, you may want to take your scissors and trim the area around the penis. With the girls, trim some of the hair around the vulva.

Now that your dog is brushed out, comb through the coat with your metal comb. By now you

The hair on the chest may be neatened with scissors.

A highly magnified top coat and undercoat hair sample from a healthy West Highland White Terrier. The thick hair is coarse with a heavy cuticle (outer sheathing). The fine hair is soft with a completely different cuticle when compared with the outer coat.

S.E.M. BY DR. DENNIS KUNKEL, UNIVERSITY OF HAWAII

have removed a fair amount of dead hair and your dog will already be looking better. You may find some small mats and these can be worked out with your fingers or your comb. If you brush your dog out every week or so, you will not have too much of a problem with mats.

We are now at the stage where you will take your clippers in hand. Your dog will only need to be clipped every three months or so, but you may want to touch up the head more often. Start with the head and follow this pattern: Take your clippers and clip the neck, shoulders and body. Be sure to trim in the direction that the hair lies. Now, take your comb and comb the leg hair down toward the table.

Take your scissors and trim the legs neatly. You can also trim off anything that "sticks out." If

A slicker brush is used to groom the Westie's top coat. A well-trained dog will withstand any amount of preparation for the show ring.

this is your first experience, you may be a bit clumsy, but the hair will grow back in a short time. The finished product may not be quite what you had expected, but expertise will come with experience and you will soon be very proud of your efforts. Your dog should now look like a West Highland White Terrier.

Put your dog in the bathtub when you are finished and give him a good bath and rinsing. After toweling him down, return him to the grooming table and trim the toenails on all four legs. At this point, you can dry your dog with a hair dryer and brush him out again. Or, you can let him dry naturally and then brush him out.

If you have grooming

DOG SOAP, PLEASE

The use of human soap products like shampoo, bubble bath and hand soap can be damaging to a dog's coat and skin. Human products are too strong and remove the protective oils coating the dog's hair and skin (making him water-resistant). Use only shampoo made especially for dogs. You also may like to use a medicated shampoo which will always help to keep external parasites at bay and is soothing to the dog's skin.

Dry your Westie as thoroughly as possible before you remove him from the tub. Once he is placed on the floor, stand back, as he is destined to shake vigorously to rid the water from his coat.

problems, you can take your dog to the professional groomer for the first couple of times to be groomed. The groomer will "set" the pattern and then it will be easier for you to get the Westie look by following the pattern that is already set in the coat. (Of course, you can eliminate all of the grooming for yourself, except for the weekly brushing, if you take your dog to the groomer every three months!) If the coat totally grows out before you start to groom, the pattern will be lost and then you will have to start over again. Just remember, many pet owners can do a much better job trimming their dogs than some professional groomers.

To wrap it up: Your pet should be brushed weekly and bathed as needed. Trim the toenails every month or so and plan to clip the dog every three months. Follow this plan and your dog will be clean, he will have a new outfit every three months and he will look like a West Highland White Terrier!

BATHING BEAUTY

Once you are sure that the dog is thoroughly rinsed, squeeze the excess water out of the coat with your hand and dry him with a heavy towel. You may choose to use a hair dryer on his coat or just let it dry naturally. In cold weather, never allow your dog outside with a wet coat.

There are "dry bath" products on the market, which are sprays and powders intended for spot cleaning that can be used between regular baths, if necessary. They are not substitutes for regular baths, but they are easy to use for touch-ups as they do not require rinsing.

Purchase a toothpaste made for dogs and brush your Westie's teeth at least once a week. This does wonders for his teeth and his breath!

EAR CLEANING

The ears should be kept clean and any excess hair inside the ear should be trimmed. Ears can be cleaned with a cotton ball and special cleaner or ear powder made especially for dogs. Be on the lookout for any signs of infection or ear-mite infestation. If your West Highland White Terrier has been shaking his head or scratching at his ears frequently, this usually indicates a problem. If his ears have an unusual odor, this is a sure sign of mite infestation or infection and a signal to have his ears checked by the veterinarian.

NAIL CLIPPING

Your West Highland White Terrier should be accustomed to having his nails trimmed at an early age, since it will be part of your maintenance routine throughout his life. Not only does it look nicer, but a dog with long nails can cause injury if he jumps up or scratches someone unintentionally. Also, a long nail has a better chance of ripping and bleeding, or causing the feet to spread. A good rule of thumb is that if you can

Excess hairs inside the ears should be carefully trimmed with scissors.

The nails are cut with a special dog nail clipper.

hear your dog's nails' clicking on the floor when he walks, his nails are too long.

Before you start cutting, make sure you can identify the "quick" in each nail. The quick is a blood vessel that runs through the center of each nail and grows rather close to the end. It will bleed if accidentally cut, which will be quite painful for the dog as it contains nerve endings. Keep some type of clotting agent on

Clean the ears with a cotton ball, as the cotton swab, shown here, can be dangerous.

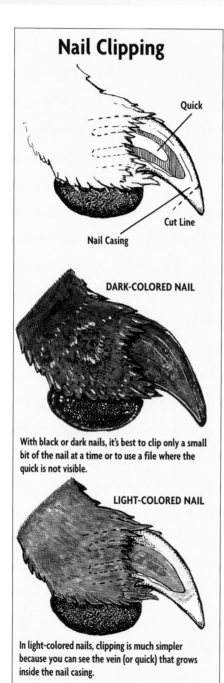

Nail Clipping

Quick

Cut Line

Nail Casing

DARK-COLORED NAIL

With black or dark nails, it's best to clip only a small bit of the nail at a time or to use a file where the quick is not visible.

LIGHT-COLORED NAIL

In light-colored nails, clipping is much simpler because you can see the vein (or quick) that grows inside the nail casing.

PEDICURE TIPS
A dog that spends a lot of time outside on a hard surface such as cement or pavement will have his nails naturally worn down and may not need to have them trimmed as often, except maybe in the colder months when he is not outside as much. Regardless, it is best to get your dog accustomed to this procedure at an early age so that he is used to it. Some dogs are especially sensitive about having their feet touched, but if a dog has experienced it since he was young, he should not be bothered by it.

hand, such as a styptic pencil or styptic powder (the type used for shaving). This will stop the bleeding quickly when applied to the end of the cut nail. Do not panic if this happens, just stop the bleeding and talk soothingly to your dog. Once he has calmed down, move on to the next nail. It is better to clip a little at a time, particularly with black-nailed dogs.

Hold your pup steady as you begin trimming his nails; you do not want him to make any sudden movements or run away. Talk to him soothingly and stroke his coat as you clip. Holding his foot in your hand, simply take off the end of each nail in one quick clip. You can purchase nail clippers that are specially made for dogs; you can

HEAT-STROKE WARNING
Never leave your dog alone in the car. In hot weather, your dog can die from the high temperature inside a closed vehicle; even a car parked in the shade can heat up very quickly. Leaving the window open is dangerous as well since the dog can hurt himself trying to get out.

Whether traveling around town or across country, the proper way to transport any dog is in a crate in the rear of the vehicle.

probably find them wherever you buy grooming supplies.

TRAVELING WITH YOUR DOG
CAR TRAVEL
You should accustom your West Highland White Terrier to riding in a car at an early age. You may or may not take him in the car often, but at the very least he will need to go to the vet and you do not want these trips to be traumatic for the dog or a big hassle for you. The safest way for a dog to ride in the car is in his crate. If he uses a fiberglass crate in the house, you can use the same crate for travel. Wire crates can be used for travel, but fiberglass or wooden crates are safer.

Put the pup in the crate and see how he reacts. If he seems uneasy, you can have a passenger hold him on his lap while you drive. Another option is a specially made safety harness for dogs, which straps the dog in much like

a seat belt. Do not let the dog roam loose in the vehicle—this is very dangerous! If you should stop short, your dog can be thrown and injured. If the dog starts climbing on you and pestering you while you are driving, you will not be able to concentrate on the road. It is an unsafe situation for everyone—human and canine.

For long trips, be prepared to stop to let the dog relieve himself. Bring along whatever you need to clean up after him. You should bring along some paper towels and old bath towels, should he have an accident in the car or become carsick.

The crate is the safest way to travel by car with your Westie. Traveling unrestrained in a car with open windows can be potentially dangerous.

A well-traveled Westie is a special companion that is adaptable and ready for anything. This little Scotsman is ready for his European tour!

him. Do not feed the dog for several hours before checking in to minimize his need to relieve himself. However, certain regulations may require you to provide the necessary items for an airline employee to feed and water your dog during stopovers on long trips.

Make sure your dog is properly identified and that your contact information appears on his ID tags and on his crate. Animals travel in a different area of the plane than human passengers and, although transporting animals is fairly routine for most major airlines, there is always the slight risk of getting separated from your dog.

VACATIONS AND BOARDING

So you want to take a family vacation—and you want to include *all* members of the family. You would probably make

AIR TRAVEL

If bringing your dog on a flight, you will have to contact the airline to make special arrangements. Every airline has different requirements and regulations, so be thorough when making plans. The dog will be required to travel in a fiberglass crate; you may be able to use your own or the airline can supply one. To help the dog be at ease, put one of his favorite toys in the crate with

TRAVEL ABROAD

For international travel you will have to make arrangements well in advance (perhaps months), as countries' regulations pertaining to bringing in animals differ. There may be special health certificates and/or vaccinations that your dog will need before taking the trip, sometimes this has to be done within a certain time frame. In rabies-free countries, you will need to bring proof of the dog's rabies vaccination and there may be a quarantine period upon arrival.

LOST AND FOUND

If your dog gets lost, he is not able to ask for directions home.

Identification tags fastened to the collar give important information—the dog's name, the owner's name, the owner's address and a telephone number where the owner can be reached. This makes it easy for whoever finds the dog to contact the owner and arrange to have the dog returned.

An added advantage is that a person will be more likely to approach a lost dog who has ID tags on his collar; it tells the person that this is somebody's pet rather than a stray. This is the easiest and fastest method of identification provided that the tags stay on the collar and the collar stays on the dog.

arrangements for accommodations ahead of time anyway, but this is especially important when traveling with a dog. You do not want to make an overnight stop at the only place around for miles and find out that they do not allow dogs. Also, you do not want to reserve a place for your family without confirming that you are traveling with a dog because if it is against their policy you may not have a place to stay.

Alternatively, if you are traveling and choose not to bring your West Highland White Terrier, you will have to make arrangements for him while you are away. Some options are to bring him to a neighbor's house to stay while you

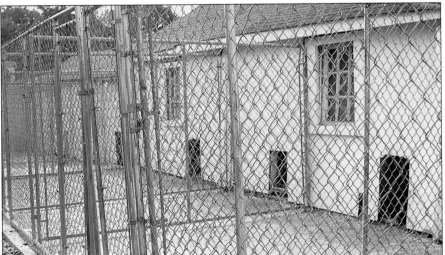

Your Westie will probably be much happier and safer in a first-rate dog kennel than traveling with you on a long trip.

are gone, to have a trusted neighbor stop by often or stay at your house or bring your dog to a reputable boarding kennel. If you choose to board him at a kennel, you should stop by to see the facility and where the dogs are kept to make sure that it is clean. Talk to some of the employees and see how they treat the dogs—do they spend time with the dogs, play with them, exercise them, etc.? You know that your West Highland White Terrier will not be happy unless he gets regular activity. Also find out the kennel's policy on vaccinations and what they require. This is for all of the dogs' safety, since when dogs are kept together there is a greater risk of diseases being passed from dog to dog.

IDENTIFICATION

Your West Highland White Terrier is your valued companion and friend. That is why you always keep a close eye on him and you have made sure that he cannot escape from your yard or wriggle out of his collar and run away from you. However, accidents can happen and there may come a time when your dog unexpectedly gets separated from you. If this unfortunate event should occur, the first thing on your mind will be finding him. Proper identification, including an ID tag, a tattoo and possibly a microchip, will increase the chances of his being returned to you safely and quickly.

IDENTIFICATION OPTIONS

As puppies become more and more expensive, especially those puppies of high quality for showing and/or breeding, they have a greater chance of being stolen. The usual collar dog tag is, of course, easily removed. But there are two more permanent techniques that have become widely used for identification.

The puppy microchip implantation involves the injection of a small microchip, about the size of a corn kernel, under the skin of the dog. If your dog shows up at a clinic or shelter, or is offered for resale under less-than-savory circumstances, it can be positively identified by the microchip. The microchip is scanned, and a registry quickly identifies you as the owner.

Tattooing is done on various parts of the dog, from his belly to his ears. The number tattooed can be your telephone number, your dog's registration number or any other number that you can easily memorize. When professional dog thieves see a tattooed dog, they usually lose interest. For the safety of our dogs, no laboratory facility or dog broker will accept a tattooed dog as stock.

Discuss microchipping and tattooing with your veterinarian and breeder. Some vets perform these services on their own premises for a reasonable fee. To ensure that your dog's identification is effective, be certain that the dog is then properly registered with a legitimate national database.

POISONOUS PLANTS

Below is a partial list of plants that are considered poisonous. These plants can cause skin irritation, illness and even death. You should be aware of the types of plants that grow in your garden and that you keep in your home. Special care should be taken to rid your garden of dangerous plants and to keep all plants in the household out of your West Highland White Terrier's reach.

American Blue Flag	Japanese Yew
Bachelor's Button	Jerusalem Cherry
Barberry	Jimson Weed
Bog Iris	Lenten Rose
Boxwood	Lily of the Valley
Buttercup	Marigold
Cherry Pits	Milkwort
Chinese Arbor	Mistletoe (berries)
Chokecherry	Monkshood
Christmas Rose	Mullein
Climbing Lily	Narcissus
Crown of Thorns	Peony
Elderberry (berries)	Persian Ivy
Elephant Ear	Rhododendron
English Ivy	Rhubarb
False Acacia	Shallon
Fern	Siberian Iris
Foxglove	Solomon's Seal
Hellebore	Star of Bethlehem
Herb of Grace	Water Lily
Holly	Wood Spurge
Horse Chestnut	Wisteria
Iris (bulb)	Yew

Canine Development Schedule

It is important to understand how and at what age a puppy develops into adulthood. If you are a puppy owner, consult the following Canine Development Schedule to determine the stage of development your West Highland White Terrier puppy is currently experiencing. This knowledge will help you as you work with the puppy in the weeks and months ahead.

Period	Age	Characteristics
FIRST TO THIRD	BIRTH TO SEVEN WEEKS	Puppy needs food, sleep and warmth, and responds to simple and gentle touching. Needs mother for security and disciplining. Needs littermates for learning and interacting with other dogs. Pup learns to function within a pack and learns pack order of dominance. Begin socializing with adults and children for short periods. Begins to become aware of its environment.
FOURTH	EIGHT TO TWELVE WEEKS	Brain is fully developed. Needs socializing with outside world. Remove from mother and littermates. Needs to change from canine pack to human pack. Human dominance necessary. Fear period occurs between 8 and 16 weeks. Avoid fright and pain.
FIFTH	THIRTEEN TO SIXTEEN WEEKS	Training and formal obedience should begin. Less association with other dogs, more with people, places, situations. Period will pass easily if you remember this is pup's change-to-adolescence time. Be firm and fair. Flight instinct prominent. Permissiveness and over-disciplining can do permanent damage. Praise for good behavior.
JUVENILE	FOUR TO EIGHT MONTHS	Another fear period about 7 to 8 months of age. It passes quickly, but be cautious of fright and pain. Sexual maturity reached. Dominant traits established. Dog should understand sit, down, come and stay by now.

NOTE: THESE ARE APPROXIMATE TIME FRAMES. ALLOW FOR INDIVIDUAL DIFFERENCES IN PUPPIES.

WEST HIGHLAND WHITE TERRIER

Living with an untrained dog is a lot like owning a piano that you do not know how to play—it is a nice object to look at but it does not do much more than that to bring you pleasure. Now try taking piano lessons and suddenly the piano comes alive and brings forth magical sounds and rhythms that set your heart singing and your body swaying.

The same is true with your West Highland White Terrier. At first you enjoy seeing him around the house. He does not do much with you other than to need food, water and exercise. Come to think of it, he does not bring you much joy, either. He is a big responsi-bility with a very small return. Often he develops unacceptable behaviors that annoy and/or infuriate you, to say nothing of bad habits that may end up costing you great sums of money. Not a good thing!

Well-trained Westies that respect your wishes and obey your commands are a joy for their entire lifetimes. Westies are very intelligent and extremely trainable.

LASTING REWARDS

If you start with a normal, healthy dog and give him time, patience and some carefully executed lessons, you will reap the rewards of that training for the life of the dog. And what a life it will be! The two of you will find immeasurable pleasure in the companionship you have built together with love, respect and understanding. Good luck and enjoy!

Now train your West Highland White Terrier. Enroll in an obedience class. Teach him good manners as you learn how and why he behaves the way he does. Find out how to communicate with your dog and how to recognize and understand his communications with you. Suddenly the dog takes on a new role in your life—he is smart, interesting, well behaved and fun to be with. He demonstrates his bond of devotion to you daily. In other words, your Westie does wonders for your ego because he constantly reminds you that you are not only his leader, you are his hero! Miraculous things have happened—you have a wonderful dog (even your family and friends have noticed the transformation!) and you feel good about yourself.

Those involved with teaching dog obedience and counseling owners about their dogs' behavior have discovered some interesting facts about dog ownership. For example, training dogs when they are puppies results in the highest rate of success in developing well-

EDUCATION PAYS OFF
Taking your dog to an obedience school may be the best investment in time and money you can ever make. You will enjoy the benefits for the lifetime of your dog and you will have the opportunity to meet people with similar expectations for their companion dogs.

mannered and well-adjusted adult dogs. Training an older dog, from six months to six years of age, can produce almost equal results, providing that the owner accepts the dog's slower rate of learning capability and is willing to work patiently to help the dog succeed at developing to his fullest potential. Unfortunately, many owners of untrained adult dogs lack the patience factor, so they do not persist until their dogs are successful at learning particular behaviors.

Training a puppy aged 8 to 16 weeks (20 weeks at the most) is like working with a dry sponge in a pool of water. The pup soaks up whatever you show him and constantly looks for more things to do and learn. At this early age, his body is not yet producing hormones, and therein lies the reason for such a high rate of success. Without hormones, he is focused on his owners and not particularly interested in investi-

Grooming and training your Wesie go hand in hand. Accepting limits and discipline helps to mold the Westie into an obedient, pliable companion.

gating other places, dogs, people, etc. You are his leader: his provider of food, water, shelter and security. He latches onto you and wants to stay close. He will usually follow you from room to room, will not let you out of his sight when you are outdoors with him and will respond in like manner to the people and animals you encounter. If you greet a friend warmly, he will be happy to greet the person as well. If, however, you are hesitant or anxious about the approach of a stranger, he will respond accordingly.

Once the puppy begins to produce hormones, his natural curiosity emerges and he begins to investigate the world around him. It is at this time when you may notice that the untrained dog begins to wander away from you and even ignore your commands to stay close. When this behavior becomes a problem, the owner has two choices: get rid of the dog or train him. It is strongly urged that you choose the latter option.

Occasionally there are no classes available within a reasonable distance from the owner's home. Sometimes there are classes available but the tuition is too costly. Whatever the circumstances, the solution to training your dog without formal classes lies within the pages of this book.

This chapter is devoted to helping you train your West Highland White Terrier at home. If

As the puppy gets older, it becomes more mature and, if not properly trained, can become unruly and even disrespectful.

KEEP SMILING
Never train your dog, puppy or adult, when you are mad or in a sour mood. Dogs are very sensitive to human feelings, especially anger, and if your dog senses that you are angry or upset, he will connect your anger with his training and learn to resent or fear his training sessions.

respond favorably to gentle motivational methods and sincere praise and encouragement. Now let us get started.

HOUSEBREAKING

You can train your puppy to relieve himself wherever you choose. For example, city dwellers often train their puppies to relieve themselves in the gutter because large plots of grass are not readily available. Suburbanites, on the other hand, usually have yards to accommodate their dogs' needs.

Outdoor training includes such surfaces as grass, dirt and cement. Indoor training usually means training your dog to newspaper.

When deciding on the surface and location that you will want your West Highland White Terrier to use, be sure it is going to be permanent. Training your dog to grass and then changing your mind two months later is extremely difficult for both dog and owner.

Next, choose the command you will use each and every time you want your puppy to void. "Go hurry up" and "Go potty" are examples of commands commonly used by dog owners.

Get in the habit of asking the puppy, "Do you want to go hurry up?" (or whatever your chosen relief command is) before you take him out. That way, when he becomes an adult, you will be

You certainly want to train your Westie to relieve himself outside...but did you really want him to use your flower bed? the recommended procedures are followed faithfully, you may expect positive results that will prove rewarding to both you and your dog.

Whether your new charge is a puppy or a mature adult, the methods of teaching and the techniques we use in training basic behaviors are the same. After all, no dog, whether puppy or adult, likes harsh or inhumane methods. All creatures, however,

TAKE THE LEAD

Do not carry your dog to his relief area. Lead him there on a leash or, better yet, encourage him to follow you to the spot. If you start carrying him to his spot, you might end up doing this routine forever and your dog will have the satisfaction of having trained *you*.

HOW MANY TIMES A DAY?

AGE	RELIEF TRIPS
To 14 weeks	10
14–22 weeks	8
22–32 weeks	6
Adulthood	4
(dog stops growing)	

These are estimates, of course, but they are a guide to the *minimum* number of opportunities a dog should have each day to relieve itself.

able to determine if he wants to go out when you ask him. A confirmation will be signs of interest, such as wagging his tail, watching you intently, going to the door, etc.

PUPPY'S NEEDS

Puppy needs to relieve himself after play periods, after each meal, after he has been sleeping and any time he indicates that he is looking for a place to urinate or defecate.

The urinary and intestinal tract muscles of very young puppies are not fully developed. Therefore, like human babies, puppies need to relieve themselves frequently.

Take your puppy out often—every hour for an eight-week-old, for example. The older the puppy, the less often he will need to relieve himself. Finally, as a mature healthy adult, he will require only three to five relief trips per day.

HOUSING

Since the types of housing and control you provide for your puppy have a direct relationship on the success of house-training, we consider the various aspects of both before we begin training.

Bringing a new puppy home and turning him loose in your house can be compared to turning a child loose in a sports arena and telling the child that the place is all his! The sheer enormity of the place would be too much for him to handle.

Instead, offer the puppy clearly defined areas where he can play, sleep, eat and live. A room of the

"Is it time to go out yet?" This Westie wants to be let out so he can relieve himself. Don't test your Westie's body control by leaving him alone for hours on end.

During the housebreaking process, the puppy will need to be taken outside frequently. Never leave a puppy outside without proper supervision.

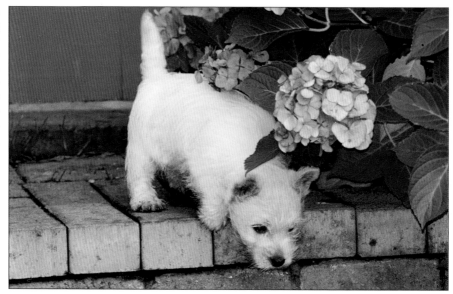

house where the family gathers is the most obvious choice. Puppies are social animals and need to feel a part of the pack right from the start. Hearing your voice, watching you while you are doing things and smelling you nearby are all positive reinforcers that he is now a member of your pack. Usually a family room, the kitchen or a nearby adjoining breakfast nook is ideal for providing safety and security for both puppy and owner.

Within that room, there should be a smaller area that the puppy can call his own. A cubbyhole, a wire or fiberglass dog crate or a fenced (not boarded!) corner from which he can view the activities of his new family will be fine. The size of the area or crate is the key factor here.

The area must be large enough for the puppy to lie down and stretch out as well as stand up without rubbing his head on the top, yet small enough so that he cannot

PAPER CAPER

Never line your pup's sleeping area with newspaper. Puppy litters are usually raised on newspaper and, once in your home, the puppy will immediately associate newspaper with voiding. Never put newspaper on any floor while house-training, as this will only confuse the puppy. If you are paper-training him, use paper in his designated relief area *only*. Finally, restrict water intake after evening meals. Offer a few licks at a time—never let a young puppy gulp water after meals.

relieve himself at one end and sleep at the other without coming into contact with his droppings.

Dogs are, by nature, clean animals and will not remain close to their relief areas unless forced to do so. In those cases, they then become dirty dogs and usually remain that way for life.

The crate or cubby should be lined with a clean towel and offer one toy, no more. Do not put food or water in the crate, as eating and drinking will activate his digestive processes and ultimately defeat your purpose as well as make the puppy very uncomfortable as he attempts to "hold it."

CONTROL

By control, we mean helping the puppy to create a lifestyle pattern that will be compatible to that of his human pack *(you!)*. Just as we guide little children to learn our way of life, we must show the puppy when it is time to play, eat, sleep, exercise and even entertain himself.

Your puppy should always sleep in his crate. He should also learn that, during times of household confusion and excessive human activity such as at breakfast when family members are preparing for the day, he can play by himself in relative safety and comfort in his crate. Each time you leave the puppy alone, he should be crated. Puppies are chewers.

Don't carry your Westie to his designated relief area. Let him walk there by himself on his leash.

They cannot tell the difference between lamp cords, television wires, shoes, table legs, etc. Chewing into a television wire, for example, can be fatal to the puppy, while a shorted wire can start a fire in the house.

If the puppy chews on the arm of the chair when he is alone, you will probably discipline him angrily when you get home. Thus, he makes the

CONSISTENCY LEADS TO SUCCESS

Most of all, be consistent. Always take your dog to the same location, always use the same command and always have him on lead when he is in his relief area, unless a fenced-in yard is available.

By following the Success Method, your puppy will be completely house-trained by the time his muscle and brain development reach maturity. Keep in mind that small breeds usually mature faster than large breeds, but all puppies should be trained by six months of age.

association that your coming home means he is going to be punished. (He will not remember chewing up the chair and is incapable of making the association of the discipline with his naughty deed.)

Other times of excitement, such as family parties, etc., can be fun for the puppy, providing he can view the activities from the security of his crate. He is not underfoot and he is not being fed all sorts of tidbits that will probably cause him stomach distress, yet he still feels a part of the fun.

SCHEDULE

A puppy should be taken to his relief area each time he is released from his crate, after meals, after a play session and when he first

---

PLAN TO PLAY

The puppy should also have regular play and exercise sessions when he is with you or a family member. Exercise for a very young puppy can consist of a short walk around the house or yard. Playing can include fetching games with a large ball or a special toy. (All puppies teethe and need soft things upon which to chew.) Remember to restrict play periods to indoors within his living area (the family room for example) until he is completely house-trained.

---

awakens in the morning (at age eight weeks, this can mean 5 a.m.!). The puppy will indicate that he's ready "to go" by circling or sniffing busily—do not misinterpret these signs. For a puppy less than ten weeks of age, a routine of taking him out every hour is necessary. As the puppy grows, he will be able to wait for longer periods of time.

Keep trips to his relief area short. Stay no more than five or six minutes and then return to the house. If he goes during that time, praise him lavishly and take him indoors immediately. If he does not, but he has an accident when you go back indoors, pick him up immediately, say "No! No!" and return to his relief area. Wait a few minutes, then return to the house again. Never hit a puppy or rub his face in urine or excrement when he has an accident!

Once indoors, put the puppy in his crate until you have had time to clean up his accident. Then release him to the family area and watch him more closely than before. Chances are, his accident was a result of your not picking up his signal or waiting too long before offering him the opportunity to relieve himself. Never hold a grudge against the puppy for accidents.

Let the puppy learn that going outdoors means it is time to relieve himself, not play. Once trained, he will be able to

The exercise needs
of a Westie
include daily walks
as well as a good
romp around your
yard.

play indoors and out and still differentiate between the times for play versus the times for relief.

Help him develop regular hours for naps, being alone, playing by himself and just resting, all in his crate. Encourage him to entertain himself while you are busy with your activities. Let him learn that having you near is comforting, but it is not your main purpose in life to provide him with your undivided attention.

Each time you put a puppy in his crate tell him, "Crate time!" (or whatever command you choose). Soon, he will run to his crate when he hears you say those words.

In the beginning of his training, do not leave him in his crate for prolonged periods of time except during the night when everyone is sleeping. Make his experience with his crate a pleasant one and, as an adult, he will love his crate and willingly stay in it for several hours. There are millions of people who go to work every day and leave their adult dogs crated while they are away. The dogs accept this as their lifestyle and look forward to "crate time."

Crate training provides safety for you, the puppy and the home. It also provides the puppy with a feeling of security and that helps the puppy achieve self-confidence and clean habits.

Remember that one of the primary ingredients in house-training your puppy is control. Regardless of your lifestyle, there will always be occasions when you will need to have a place where your dog can stay and be happy and safe. Crate training is the answer for now and in the future.

In conclusion, a few key elements are really all you need for a successful house-training method—consistency, frequency, praise, control and supervision. By following these procedures with a normal, healthy puppy, you and the puppy will soon be past the stage of "accidents" and ready to move on to a full and rewarding life together.

THE SUCCESS METHOD

Success that comes by luck is usually short-lived. Success that comes by well-thought-out proven methods is often more easily achieved and permanent. This is the Success Method. It is designed to give you, the puppy owner, a simple yet proven way to help your puppy develop clean living habits and a feeling of security in his new environment.

6 Steps to Successful Crate Training

1 Tell the puppy "Crate time!" and place him in the crate with a small treat (a piece of cheese or half of a biscuit). Let him stay in the crate for five minutes while you are in the same room. Then release him and praise lavishly. Never release him when he is fussing. Wait until he is quiet before you let him out.

2 Repeat Step 1 several times a day.

3 The next day, place the puppy in the crate as before. Let him stay there for ten minutes. Do this several times.

4 Continue building time in five-minute increments until the puppy stays in his crate for 30 minutes with you in the room. Always take him to his relief area after prolonged periods in his crate.

5 Now go back to Step 1 and let the puppy stay in his crate for five minutes, this time while you are out of the room.

6 Once again, build crate time in five-minute increments with you out of the room. When the puppy will stay willingly in his crate (he may even fall asleep!) for 30 minutes with you out of the room, he will be ready to stay in it for several hours at a time.

ROLES OF DISCIPLINE, REWARD AND PUNISHMENT

Discipline, training one to act in accordance with rules, brings order to life. It is as simple as that. Without discipline, particularly in a group society, chaos reigns supreme and the group will eventually perish. Humans and canines are social animals and need some form of discipline in order to function effectively. They must procure food, protect their home base and their young and reproduce to keep the species going.

If there were no discipline in

Once your Westie is acclimated to his crate and completely housebroken, he will enjoy both exploring his designated area in the house and his time in the privacy of his crate.

PRACTICE MAKES PERFECT!

- Have training lessons with your dog every day in several short segments—three to five times a day for a few minutes at a time is ideal.
- Do not have long practice sessions. The dog will become easily bored.
- Never practice when you are tired, ill, worried or in an otherwise negative mood. This will transmit to the dog and may have an adverse effect on its performance.

Think fun, short and, above all, *positive!* End each session on a high note, rather than a failed exercise, and make sure to give a lot of praise. Enjoy the training and help your dog enjoy it, too.

---

the lives of social animals, they would eventually die from starvation and/or predation by other stronger animals.

In the case of domestic canines, dogs need discipline in their lives in order to understand how their pack (you and other family members) functions and how they must act in order to survive.

A large humane society in a highly populated area recently surveyed dog owners regarding their satisfaction with their relationships with their dogs. People who had trained their dogs were 75% more satisfied with their pets than those who had never trained their dogs.

Dr. Edward Thorndike, a psychologist, established

Rewards and praise are more effective in training than punishment. Although your Westie should behave to please you, an occasional bribe does wonders.

Thorndike's Theory of Learning, which states that a behavior that results in a pleasant event tends to be repeated. A behavior that results in an unpleasant event tends not to be repeated. It is this theory on which training methods are based today. For example, if you manipulate a dog to perform a specific behavior and reward him for doing it, he is likely to do it again because he enjoyed the end result.

Occasionally, punishment, a penalty inflicted for an offense, is necessary. The best type of punishment often comes from an outside source. For example, a child is told not to touch the stove because he may get burned. He disobeys and touches the stove. In doing so, he receives a burn. From that time on, he respects the heat of the stove and avoids contact with it. Therefore, a behavior that results in an unpleasant event tends not to be repeated.

A good example of a dog's learning the hard way is the dog who chases the house cat. He is told many times to leave the cat

Your Westie's identification tags should be securely attached to his collar at all times.

alone, yet he persists in teasing the cat. Then, one day he begins chasing the cat but the cat turns and swipes a claw across the dog's face, leaving him with a painful gash on his nose. The final result is that the dog stops chasing the cat.

TRAINING EQUIPMENT
COLLAR
A simple buckle collar is fine for most dogs. One who pulls mightily on the leash may require a chain choker collar. You, as the dog's trainer, must be completely comfortable with the training equipment you choose. Your Westie's training collar must fit snugly but not too tightly.

LEASH
A 1- to 2-yard leash is recommended, preferably made of leather, nylon or heavy cloth. A chain leash is not recommended, as many dog owners find that the chain cuts into their hands and that frequently switching the leash back and forth between their hands is painful.

CHOOSE AN APPROPRIATE COLLAR

The **BUCKLE COLLAR** is the standard collar used for everyday purposes. Be sure that you adjust the buckle on growing puppies. Check it every day. It can become too tight overnight! These collars can be made of leather or nylon. Attach your dog's identification tags to this collar.

The **CHOKE COLLAR** is designed for training. It is constructed of highly polished steel so that it slides easily through the stainless steel loop. The idea is that the dog controls the pressure around his neck and he will stop pulling if the collar becomes uncomfortable. It should *not* be used on the Westie.

The **HALTER** is for a trained dog that has to be restrained to prevent running away, chasing a cat and the like. Considered the most humane of all collars, it is frequently used on smaller dogs on which collars are not comfortable.

Nylon leashes are popular for everyday use. You should always walk your Westie on a leash, especially when he will be meeting other dogs.

TREATS

Have a bag of treats on hand. Something nutritious and easy to swallow works best. Use a soft treat, a chunk of cheese or a piece of cooked chicken rather than a dry biscuit. By the time the dog gets done chewing a dry treat, will forget why he is being rewarded in the first place! Using food rewards will not teach a dog to beg at the table—the only way to teach a dog to beg at the table is to give him food from the table. In training, rewarding the dog with a food treat will help him associate praise and the treats with learning new behaviors that obviously please his owner.

TRAINING BEGINS: ASK THE DOG A QUESTION

In order to teach your dog anything, you must first get his attention. After all, he cannot learn anything if he is looking

GOLDEN RULE

The golden rule of dog training is simple. For each "question" (command), there is only one correct answer (reaction). One command = one reaction. Keep practicing the command until the dog reacts correctly without hesitating. Be repetitive but not monotonous. Dogs get bored just as people do!

PARENTAL GUIDANCE

Training a dog is a life experience. Many parents admit that much of what they know about raising children they learned from caring for their dogs. Dogs respond to love, fairness and guidance, just as children do. Become a good dog owner and you may become an even better parent—and your Westie doesn't need a college fund!

What dog doesn't love a snack? Using food as a training aid is often helpful in teaching new commands.

away from you with his mind on something else.

To get his attention, ask him, "School?" and immediately walk over to him and give him a treat as you tell him "Good dog." Wait

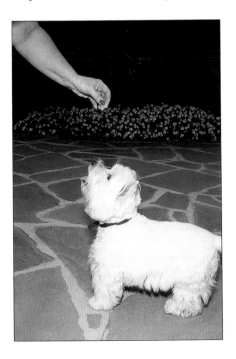

a minute or two and repeat the routine, this time with a treat in your hand as you approach within a foot of the dog. Do not go directly to him, but stop about a foot short of him and hold out the treat as you ask, "School?" He will see you approaching with a treat in your hand and most likely begin walking toward you. As you meet, give him the treat and praise again.

The third time, ask the question, have a treat in your hand and walk only a short distance toward the dog so that he must walk almost all the way to

Before you can teach your dog anything, you must have his attention... a food treat does wonders in making your Westie take notice!

Placing light pressure on the dog's hindquarters will help ease him into the sit position as you are teaching the exercise.

THE BASIC COMMANDS
TEACHING SIT

Now that you have the dog's attention, attach his leash and hold it in your left hand and a food treat in your right. Place your food hand at the dog's nose and let him lick the treat but not take it from you. Say "Sit" and slowly raise your food hand from in front of the dog's nose up over his head so that he is looking at the ceiling. As he bends his head upward, he will have to bend his knees to maintain his balance. As he bends his knees, he will assume a sit position. At that point, release the food treat and praise lavishly with comments such as "Good dog! Good sit!", etc. Remember to always praise enthusiastically, because dogs relish verbal praise from their owners and feel so

you. As he reaches you, give him the treat and praise again.

By this time, the dog will probably be getting the idea that if he pays attention to you, especially when you ask that question, it will pay off in treats and fun activities for him. In other words, he learns that "school" means doing fun things with you that result in treats and positive attention for him.

Remember that the dog does not understand your verbal language, he only recognizes sounds. Your question translates to a series of sounds for him, and those sounds become the signal to go to you and pay attention; if he does, he will get to interact with you plus receive treats and praise.

LANGUAGE BARRIER
Dogs do not understand our language and have to rely on tone of voice more than just words or sound. They can be trained to react to a certain sound, at a certain volume. If you say "No, Oliver" in a very soft, pleasant voice, it will not have the same meaning as "No, Oliver!!" when you raise your voice.

You should never use the dog's name during a reprimand, just the command "No! " You never want the dog to associate his name with a negative experience or reprimand.

All dogs need discipline, and they look to their owners to provide it.

"DOGSPEAK"

Dogs are sensitive to their master's moods and emotions and the West Highland White Terrier is no exception. Use your voice wisely when communicating with your dog. Never raise your voice at your dog unless you are angry and trying to correct him. "Barking" at your dog can become as meaningless as "dogspeak" is to you. Think before you bark!

commands. Food is only used to teach new behaviors, and once the dog knows what you want when you give a specific command, you will wean him off the food treats but still maintain the verbal praise. After all, you will always have your voice with you, and there will be many times when you have no food rewards but expect the dog to obey.

TEACHING DOWN

Teaching the down exercise is easy when you understand how the dog perceives the down position, and it is very difficult when you do not. Dogs perceive the down position as a submissive one; therefore, teaching the down

proud of themselves whenever they accomplish a behavior.

You will not use food forever in getting the dog to obey your

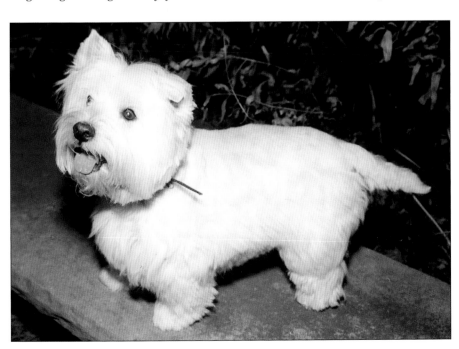

Teaching your
Westie to stay in
either the sit or
down position may
require some
patience but it is
usually not
difficult.

exercise using a forceful method can sometimes make the dog develop such a fear of the down that he either runs away when you say "Down" or he attempts to bite the person who tries to force him down.

Have the dog sit close alongside your left leg, facing in the same direction as you are. Hold the leash in your left hand and a food treat in your right. Now place your left hand lightly on the top of the dog's shoulders where they meet above the spinal cord. Do not push down on the dog's shoulders; simply rest your left hand there so you can guide the dog to lie down close to your left leg rather than to swing away

from your side when he drops.

Now place the food hand at the dog's nose, say "Down" very softly (almost a whisper), and slowly lower the food hand to the dog's front feet. When the food hand reaches the floor, begin moving it forward along the floor in front of the dog. Keep talking softly to the dog, saying things like, "Do you want this treat? You can do this, good dog." Your reassuring tone of voice will help calm the dog as he tries to follow the food hand in order to get the treat.

When the dog's elbows touch the floor, release the food and praise softly. Try to get the dog to maintain that down position for several seconds before you let him sit up again. The goal here is to get the dog to settle down and not feel threatened in the down position.

TEACHING STAY

It is easy to teach the dog to stay in either a sit or a down position. Again, we use food and praise during the teaching process as we help the dog to understand exactly what it is that we are expecting him to do.

To teach the sit/stay, start with the dog sitting on your left side as before and hold the leash in your left hand. Have a food treat in your right hand and place your food hand at the dog's nose. Say "Stay" and step out on

SELF-DEFENSE

To a dog's way of thinking, your hands are like his mouth in terms of a defense mechanism. If you squeeze him too tightly, he might just bite you because that would be his normal response. This is not aggressive biting and, although all biting should be discouraged, you need the discipline in learning how to handle your dog.

your right foot to stand directly in front of the dog, toe to toe, as he licks and nibbles the treat. Be sure to keep his head facing upward to maintain the sit position. Count to five and then swing around to stand next to the dog again with him on your left. As soon as you get back to the original position, release the food and praise lavishly.

To teach the down/stay, do the down as previously described. As soon as the dog lies down, say "Stay" and step out on your right foot just as you did in the sit/stay. Count to five and then return to stand beside the dog with him on your left side. Release the treat and praise as always.

Within a week to ten days, you can begin to add a bit of distance between you and your dog when you leave him. When you do, use your left hand open with the palm facing the dog as a stay signal, much the same as the hand signal a police officer uses to stop traffic at an intersection. Hold the food treat in your right hand as before, but this time the food is not touching the dog's nose. He will watch the food hand and quickly learn that he is going to get that treat as soon as you return to his side.

When you can stand 1 yard away from your dog for 30 seconds, you can then begin building time and distance in both stays. Eventually, the dog can be expected to remain in the stay position for prolonged periods of time until you return to him or call him to you. Always praise lavishly when he stays.

It takes about a week or two to train your Westie to stay in the desired position. This discipline must be practiced and reinforced frequently.

The "come" exercise should begin with the puppy as a game. This must be the most exciting fun for the puppy, because it is the most important of all lessons.

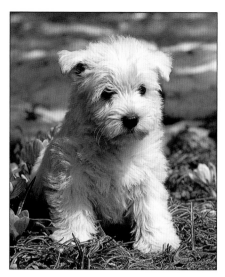

TEACHING COME

If you make teaching "come" a fun experience, you should never have a "student" that does not love the game or that fails to come when called. The secret, it seems, is never to teach the word "come."

At times when an owner most wants his dog to come when called, the owner is likely upset or anxious and he allows these feelings to come through in the tone of his voice when he calls his dog. Hearing that desperation in his owner's voice, the dog fears the results of going to him and therefore either disobeys outright or runs in the opposite direction. The secret, therefore, is to teach the dog a game and, when you want him to come to you, simply play the game. It is practically a no-fail solution!

To begin, have several members of your family take a few food treats and each go into a different room in the house. Take turns calling the dog; each person should celebrate the dog's finding him with a treat and lots of happy praise. When a person calls the dog, he is actually inviting the dog to find him and get a treat as a reward for "winning."

A few turns of the "Where are you?" game and the dog will figure out that everyone is playing the game and that each person has a big celebration awaiting his success at locating him. Once he learns to love the game, simply calling out "Where are you?" will bring him running from wherever he is when he hears that all-important question.

The come command is recognized as one of the most important things to teach a dog, but there are trainers who work with thousands of dogs and never

---

"COME"...BACK

Never call your dog to come to you for a correction or scold him when he reaches you. That is the quickest way to turn a "Come" command into "Go away fast!" Dogs think only in the present tense and he will connect the scolding with coming to his master, not with the misbehavior of a few moments earlier.

teach the actual word "come." Yet these dogs will race to respond to a person who uses the dog's name followed by "Where are you?" For example, a woman has a 12-year-old companion dog who went blind, but who never fails to locate her owner when asked, "Where are you?"

Children particularly love to play this game with their dogs. Children can hide in smaller places like a shower or bathtub, behind a bed or under a table. The dog needs to work a little bit harder to find these hiding places,

but when he does, he loves to celebrate with a treat and a tussle with a favorite youngster.

TEACHING HEEL

Heeling means that the dog walks beside the owner without pulling. It takes time and patience on the owner's part to succeed at teaching the dog that he (the owner) will not proceed unless the dog is walking calmly beside him. Pulling out ahead on the leash is definitely not acceptable.

Begin with holding the leash in your left hand as the dog sits beside your left leg. Move the loop end of the leash to your right hand but keep your left hand short on the leash so it keeps the dog in close next to you.

Say "Heel" and step forward on your left foot. Keep the dog close to you and take three steps. Stop and have the dog sit next to you in what we now call the heel position. Praise

Dogs often anticipate the trainer's next command. Make training fun and rewarding for the puppy and your success is guaranteed.

"WHERE ARE YOU?"

When calling the dog, do not say "Come." Say things like, "Rover, where are you? See if you can find me! I have a cookie for you!" Keep up a constant line of chatter with coaxing sounds and frequent questions such as, "Where are you?" The dog will learn to follow the sound of your voice to locate you and receive his reward.

This Westie has been commanded to sit/stay. He won't take his eyes from his master as he awaits the next command.

A properly trained
dog must be
taught to walk at
your pace and at
your side. Imagine
how an untrained
Westie would mis-
behave in this
parade?

verbally, but do not touch the dog. Hesitate a moment and begin again with "Heel," taking three steps and stopping, at which point the dog is told to sit again.

Your goal here is to have the dog walk those three steps without pulling on the leash. When he will walk calmly beside you for three steps without pulling, increase the number of steps you take to five. When he will walk politely

beside you while you take five steps, you can increase the length of your walk to ten steps. Keep increasing the length of your stroll until the dog will walk quietly beside you without pulling as long as you want him to heel. When you stop heeling, indicate to the dog that the exercise is over by verbally praising as you pet him and say, "OK, good dog." The "OK" is used as a release word, meaning that the exercise is finished and the dog is free to relax.

If you are dealing with a dog who insists on pulling you around, simply "put on your brakes" and stand your ground until the dog realizes that the two of you are not going anywhere until he is beside you and moving at your pace, not his. It may take some time just standing there to convince the dog that you are the leader and you will be the one to decide on the direction and speed of your travel.

Each time the dog looks up at you or slows down to give a slack leash between the two of you, quietly praise him and say, "Good heel. Good dog." Eventually, the dog will begin to respond and within a few days he will be walking politely beside you without pulling on the leash. At first, the training sessions should be kept short and very positive; soon the dog

TUG OF WALK

If you begin teaching the heel by taking long walks and letting the dog pull you along, he misinterprets this action as an acceptable form of taking a walk. When you pull back on the leash to counteract his pulling, he reads that tug as a signal to pull even harder!

HEELING WELL

Teach your dog to heel in an enclosed area. Once you think the dog will obey reliably and you want to attempt advanced obedience exercises such as off-lead heeling, test him in a fenced in area so he cannot run away.

will be able to walk nicely with you for increasingly longer distances. Remember also to give the dog free time and the opportunity to run and play when you are done with heel practice.

WEANING OFF FOOD IN TRAINING

Food is used in training new behaviors. Once the dog understands what behavior goes with a specific command, it is time to start weaning him off the food treats. At first, give a treat after each exercise. Then, start to give a treat only after every other exercise. Mix up the times when you offer a food reward and the times when you only offer praise so that the dog will never know when he is going to receive both food and praise and when he is going to receive only praise. This is called a variable ratio reward system and it

Unless on a relief break, your Westie should walk alongside you on his lead and not pull far ahead.

proves successful because there is always the chance that the owner will produce a treat, so the dog never stops trying for that reward. No matter what, *always* give verbal praise.

OBEDIENCE CLASSES

As previously discussed, it is a good idea to enroll in an obedience class if one is available in your area. Many areas have dog clubs that offer basic obedience training as well as preparatory classes for obedience competition. There are also local dog trainers who offer similar classes.

At obedience trials sponsored by the American Kennel Club or a West Highland White Terrier Club, dogs can earn titles at various levels of competition. The

BORN PRODIGY
Occasionally, a dog and owner who have not attended formal classes have been able to earn entry-level titles by obtaining competition rules and regulations from a local kennel club and practicing on their own to a degree of perfection. Obtaining the higher level titles, however, almost always require extensive training under the tutelage of experienced instructors. In addition, the more difficult levels require more specialized equipment whereas the lower levels do not.

beginning levels of competition include basic behaviors such as sit, down, heel, etc. The more advanced levels of competition include jumping, retrieving, scent discrimination and signal work. The advanced levels require a dog and owner to put a lot of time and effort into their training and the titles that can be earned at these levels of competition are very prestigious.

Westies, like most other dogs, are very food-motivated. It is sometimes difficult to quit food treats entirely, but it's helpful to practice without them sometimes.

OTHER ACTIVITIES FOR LIFE

Whether a dog is trained in the structured environment of a class or alone with his owner at home, there are many activities that can bring fun and rewards to both owner and dog once they have mastered basic control.

Teaching the dog to help out around the home, in the yard or on the farm provides great satisfaction to both dog and owner. In addition, the dog's help makes life a little easier for his owner and raises his stature as a valued companion to his family. It helps give the dog a purpose by occupying his mind and providing an outlet for his energy.

Hiking is an exciting and healthful activity that the dog can be taught without assistance from more than his owner. The exercise of walking and climbing is beneficial for man and dog alike, and the bond that they develop together is priceless.

If you are interested in participating in organized competition with your West Highland White Terrier, there are activities other than obedience in which you and your dog can become involved. Earthdog tests are every terrier's

favorite outing and these are AKC-sanctioned events. Agility is also a popular and fun sport in which dogs run through an obstacle course that includes various jumps, tunnels and other exercises to test the dog's speed and coordination. The owners run through the course beside their dogs to give commands and to guide them through the course. Although competitive, the focus is on fun—it's fun to do, fun to watch and great exercise.

Training and proper care helps to mold a biddable and reliable companion dog. Westies excel in many different disciplines, from pet around the home to competitive obedience dog.

OBEDIENCE SCHOOL

A basic obedience beginner's class usually lasts for six to eight weeks. Dog and owner attend an hour-long lesson once a week and practice for a few minutes, several times a day, each day at home. If done properly, the whole procedure will result in a well-mannered dog and an owner who delights in living with a pet that is eager to please and enjoys doing things with his owner.

WEST HIGHLAND WHITE TERRIER

Dogs suffer from many of the same physical illnesses as people. They might even share many of the same psychological problems. Since people usually know more about human diseases than canine maladies, many of the terms used in this chapter will be familiar but not necessarily those used by veterinarians. We will use the term *x-ray,* instead of the more acceptable term *radiograph.* We will also use the familiar term *symptoms* even though dogs don't have symptoms, which are verbal descriptions of the patient's feelings; dogs have *clinical signs.* Since dogs can't speak, we have to look for clinical

signs...but we still use the term *symptoms* in this book.

As a general rule, medicine is *practiced.* That term is not arbitrary. Medicine is a constantly changing art as we learn more and more about genetics, electronic aids (like CAT scans and MRIs) and daily laboratory advances. There are many dog maladies, like canine hip dysplasia, which are not universally treated in the same manner. Some veterinarians opt for surgery more often than others do.

SELECTING A VET

Your selection of a veterinarian should be based not only upon personality and proven ability but also upon his convenience to your home. You want a vet who is close because you might have emergencies or need to make multiple visits for treatments. You want a vet who has services that you might require such as a boarding kennel and grooming facilities, as well as sophisticated pet supplies and a good reputation

Establish a relationship with your chosen vet and have him examine your Westie on a regular basis. Ideally that may be every six months, but certainly not less than once a year.

for ability and responsiveness. There is nothing more frustrating than having to wait a day or more to get a response from your veterinarian.

All veterinarians are licensed and their diplomas and/or certificates should be displayed in their waiting rooms. There are, however, many veterinary specialties that usually require further studies and internships. There are specialists in heart problems (veterinary cardiologists), skin problems (veterinary dermatologists), teeth and gum problems (veterinary dentists), eye problems (veterinary ophthalmologists and x-rays (veterinary radiologists), and vets who have specialties in bones, muscles or certain organs. Most veterinarians do routine surgery such as neutering, stitching up wounds and docking tails for those breeds in which such is required for show purposes. When the problem affecting your dog is serious, it is not unusual or impudent to get another medical opinion. You might also want to compare costs among several veterinarians. Sophisticated health care and veterinary services can be very costly. Don't be bashful about discussing these costs with your veterinarian or his (her) staff. It is not infrequent that important decisions are based upon financial considerations.

If your dog starts to act abnormally and you suspect he is ill, take him to the vet for an examination. Never hesitate to call and make an appointment if your dog is sick.

PREVENTATIVE MEDICINE

It is much easier, less costly and more effective to practice preventative medicine than to fight bouts of illness and disease. Properly bred puppies come from parents that were selected based upon their genetic disease profiles. Their mothers should have been vaccinated, free of all internal and external parasites and properly nourished. For these reasons, a visit to the veterinary surgeon who cared for the dam (mother) is recommended. The dam can pass on disease resistance to her puppies, which can last for eight to ten weeks. She can also pass on parasites and many infections. That's why you should meet the dam and know about her general health.

WEANING TO FIVE MONTHS OLD

Puppies should be weaned by the time they are about two

months old. A puppy that remains for at least eight weeks with its mother and littermates usually adapts better to other dogs and people later in its life.

In every case, you should have your newly acquired puppy examined by a veterinarian immediately. Vaccination programs usually begin when the puppy is very young.

The puppy will have its teeth examined and have its skeletal conformation and general health checked prior to certification by the veterinarian. Many puppies have problems with their kneecaps, cataracts and other eye problems, heart murmurs and undescended testicles. They may also have personality problems and your veterinarian might have training in temperament evaluation.

VACCINATION SCHEDULING

Most vaccinations are given by injection and should only be done by a veterinarian. Both he and you should keep a record of the date of the injection, the identification of the vaccine

HEALTH AND VACCINATION SCHEDULE

AGE IN WEEKS:	6TH	8TH	10TH	12TH	14TH	16TH	20-24TH	52ND
Worm Control	✔	✔	✔	✔	✔	✔	✔	
Neutering							✔	
Heartworm		✔		✔		✔	✔	
Parvovirus	✔		✔		✔		✔	✔
Distemper		✔		✔		✔		✔
Hepatitis		✔		✔		✔		✔
Leptospirosis								✔
Parainfluenza	✔		✔		✔			✔
Dental Examination		✔					✔	✔
Complete Physical		✔					✔	✔
Coronavirus				✔			✔	✔
Canine Cough	✔							
Hip Dysplasia								✔
Rabies							✔	

Vaccinations are not instantly effective. It takes about two weeks for the dog's immune system to develop antibodies. Most vaccinations require annual booster shots. Your vet should guide you in this regard.

Skeleton of the West Highland White Terrier

Skull

Cervical Vertebrae

Thoracic Vertebrae

Lumbar Vertebrae

Sacrum

Coccygeal Vertebrae

Mandible

Scapula

Humerus

Sternum

Ulna

Radius

Carpus

Metacarpus

Pelvis

Femur

Patella

Fibula

Tibia

Tuber Calcis

Tarsis

Metatarsis

Phalanges

and the amount given. The first vaccinations should start when the puppy is 6–8 weeks old, the second when it is 10–12 weeks of age and the third when it is 14–16 weeks of age. Vaccinations should never be given without a 15-day lapse between injections.

Most vaccinations immunize your puppy against viruses. The usual vaccines contain immunizing doses of several different viruses such as

HOW VACCINES WORK

Vaccines do not work all the time. Sometimes dogs are allergic to them and many times the antibodies, which are supposed to be stimulated by the vaccine, just are not produced. You should keep your dog in the veterinary clinic for an hour after it is vaccinated to be sure there are no allergic reactions.

distemper, parvovirus, parainfluenza and hepatitis. There are other vaccines available when the puppy is at risk. You should rely upon professional advice. This is especially true for the booster-shot program. Most vaccination programs require a booster when the puppy is a year old and once a year thereafter. In some cases, circumstances may require more or less frequent immunizations. Canine cough, more formally known as tracheobronchitis, is treated with a vaccine that is sprayed into the dog's nostrils.

DENTAL HEALTH

A dental examination is in order when the dog is between six months and one year of age so any permanent teeth that have erupted incorrectly can be corrected. It is important to begin a brushing routine while the dog is still a puppy. Durable nylon and safe edible chews should be a part of your Westie's arsenal for good health, good teeth and pleasant breath. The vast majority of dogs three to four years old and older has diseases of their gums from lack of dental attention. Using the various types of dental chews can be very effective in controlling dental plaque.

The effectiveness of a parvovirus vaccination program can be tested using the parvovirus antibody titer to be certain that the vaccinations are protective. Your veterinarian will explain and manage all of these details.

FIVE MONTHS TO ONE YEAR

By the time your puppy is five months old, he should have completed his vaccination program. During his physical examination he should be evaluated for the common hip dysplasia and other diseases of the joints. There are tests to assist in the prediction of these problems. Other tests can be run to assess the effectiveness of the vaccination program.

Unless you intend to breed or show your dog, neutering the puppy at six months of age is recommended. Discuss this with your veterinarian; most professionals advise neutering the puppy. Neutering has proven to be extremely beneficial to both male and female puppies. Besides eliminating the possibility of pregnancy, it inhibits (but does not prevent) breast cancer in bitches and prostate cancer in male dogs.

DOGS OLDER THAN ONE YEAR

Continue to visit the veterinarian at least once a year. There is no such disease as old age, but

PROPER DIET
Feeding your dog properly is very important. An incorrect diet could affect the dog's health, behaviour and nervous system, possibly making a normal dog into an aggressive one.

bodily functions do change with age. The eyes and ears are no longer as efficient. Liver, kidney and intestinal functions often decline. Proper dietary changes, recommended by your veterinarian, can make life more pleasant for the aging West Highland White Terrier and you.

SKIN PROBLEMS IN WEST HIGHLAND WHITE TERRIERS
Veterinarians are consulted by dog owners for skin problems more than for any other group of diseases or maladies. Dogs' skin is almost as sensitive as human skin and both suffer from almost the same ailments (though the occurrence of acne in dog is rare!). For this reason, veterinary dermatology has developed into a specialty practiced by many vets.

DISEASE REFERENCE CHART

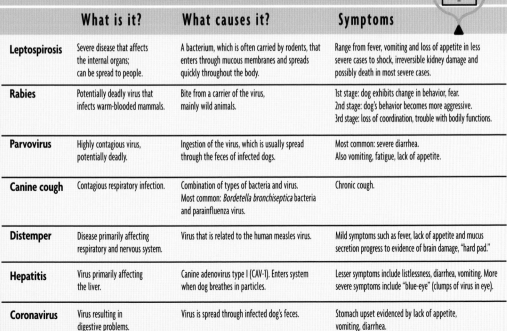

	What is it?	What causes it?	Symptoms
Leptospirosis	Severe disease that affects the internal organs; can be spread to people.	A bacterium, which is often carried by rodents, that enters through mucous membranes and spreads quickly throughout the body.	Range from fever, vomiting and loss of appetite in less severe cases to shock, irreversible kidney damage and possibly death in most severe cases.
Rabies	Potentially deadly virus that infects warm-blooded mammals.	Bite from a carrier of the virus, mainly wild animals.	1st stage: dog exhibits change in behavior, fear. 2nd stage: dog's behavior becomes more aggressive. 3rd stage: loss of coordination, trouble with bodily functions.
Parvovirus	Highly contagious virus, potentially deadly.	Ingestion of the virus, which is usually spread through the feces of infected dogs.	Most common: severe diarrhea. Also vomiting, fatigue, lack of appetite.
Canine cough	Contagious respiratory infection.	Combination of types of bacteria and virus. Most common: *Bordetella bronchiseptica* bacteria and parainfluenza virus.	Chronic cough.
Distemper	Disease primarily affecting respiratory and nervous system.	Virus that is related to the human measles virus.	Mild symptoms such as fever, lack of appetite and mucus secretion progress to evidence of brain damage, "hard pad."
Hepatitis	Virus primarily affecting the liver.	Canine adenovirus type I (CAV-1). Enters system when dog breathes in particles.	Lesser symptoms include listlessness, diarrhea, vomiting. More severe symptoms include "blue-eye" (clumps of virus in eye).
Coronavirus	Virus resulting in digestive problems.	Virus is spread through infected dog's feces.	Stomach upset evidenced by lack of appetite, vomiting, diarrhea.

HEALTH FIRST

Your veterinarian will probably recommend that your puppy be vaccinated before you take him outside. Keep in mind that there are airborne diseases, parasite eggs in the grass and unexpected visits from other dogs that might be dangerous to your puppy's health. Your West Highland White Terrier's health always comes first.

Since many skin problems have visual symptoms that are almost identical, it requires the skill of an experienced veterinary dermatologist to identify and cure many of the more severe skin disorders. Pet shops sell many treatments for skin problems but most of the treatments are directed at symptoms and not the underlying problem(s). If your dog is suffering from a skin disorder, you should seek professional assistance as quickly as possible. As with all diseases, the earlier a problem is identified and treated, the more likely is the cure.

HEREDITARY SKIN PROBLEMS
Veterinary dermatologists are currently researching a number of skin disorders that are believed to have a hereditary basis. These inherited diseases are transmitted by both parents, who appear (phenotypically) normal but have a recessive gene for the disease; meaning that they carry, but are not affected by, the disease. These diseases pose serious problems to breeders because in some instances there are no methods of identifying carriers.

Among the hereditary skin disorders, for which the mode of inheritance is known, are acrodermatitis, cutaneous asthenia (Ehlers-Danlos syndrome), sebaceous adenitis, cyclic hematopoiesis, dermato-myositis, IgA deficiency, color dilution alopecia and nodular dermatofibrosis. Some of these disorders are limited to one or two breeds, while others affect a large number of breeds. In West Highland White Terriers, epidermal dysplasia is most commonly found. Young puppies manifest dark-colored skin and are very itchy. The dark, thickened skin appears dry but greasy, like a dog suffering from bad allergies. Diagnosis is accomplished by skin biopsies and only experienced dermatologists are qualified to identify epidermal dysplasia. There is no known cure, but vets prescribe potent topical and oral medications to control the discomfort. Affected dogs (and their relatives) should not be bred.

All inherited diseases must be diagnosed and treated by a

veterinary specialist. There are active programs being undertaken by many veterinary pharmaceutical manufacturers to solve most, if not all, of the common skin problems of dogs.

PARASITE BITES

Many of us are allergic to mosquito bites. The bites itch, erupt and may even become infected. Dogs have the same reaction to fleas, ticks and/or mites. When you feel the prick of the mosquito as it bites you, you have a chance to kill it with your hand. Unfortunately, when your dog is bitten by a flea, tick or mite, it can only scratch it away or bite it. By the time the dog has been bitten, the parasite has done some of its damage. It may also have laid eggs to cause further problems in the near future. The itching from parasite bites is probably due to the saliva injected into the site when the parasite sucks the dog's blood.

AUTO-IMMUNE SKIN CONDITIONS

Auto-immune skin conditions are commonly referred to as being allergic to yourself, while allergies are usually inflammatory reactions to an outside stimulus. Auto-immune diseases cause serious damage to the tissues that are involved.

The best known auto-immune disease is lupus, which affects people as well as dogs. The symptoms are variable and may affect the kidneys, bones, blood chemistry and skin. It can be fatal to both dogs and humans, though it is not thought to be transmissible. It is usually successfully treated with cortisone, prednisone or similar corticosteroid, but extensive use of these drugs can have harmful side effects.

AIRBORNE ALLERGIES

West Highland White Terriers show greater tendency toward

A SKUNKY PROBLEM

Have you noticed your dog dragging his rump along the floor? If so, it is likely that his anal sacs are impacted or possibly infected. The anal sacs are small pouches located on both sides of the anus under the skin and muscles. They are about the size and shape of a grape and contain a foul-smelling liquid. Their contents are usually emptied when the dog has a bowel movement but, if not emptied completely, they will impact, which will cause your dog much pain. Fortunately, your veterinarian can tend to this problem easily by draining the sacs for the dog. Be aware that your dog might also empty his anal sacs in cases of extreme fright.

Of course, all dogs that spend time outdoors are potentially subject to parasite infestation, insect bites and airborne allergies.

tested for allergens. Discuss the testing with your veterinary dermatologist. Westies suffering from inflammation due to allergies tend to exhibit darker skin, developing from red to a blackish color.

FOOD PROBLEMS
FOOD ALLERGIES

inhalant allergies than other breeds. The usual offenders include pollen, dust and molds. Humans have hay fever, rose fever and other fevers from which they suffer during the pollinating season. Many dogs suffer from the same allergies. When the pollen count is high, your dog might suffer but don't expect him to sneeze and have a runny nose like a human would. Dogs react to pollen allergies the same way they react to fleas—they scratch and bite themselves. Westies tend to rub their faces with their front feet, lick and bite at their front feet and develop rashes on their bellies or in the armpits. West Highland White Terriers are very susceptible to airborne pollen and house-dust allergies, so do not think that your Westie will only encounter potential allergens outdoors.

Dogs, like humans, can be

Dogs can be allergic to many foods that are best-sellers and highly recommended by breeders and veterinarians. Changing the brand of food that you buy may not eliminate the problem if the element to which the dog is allergic is also contained in the new brand.

Recognizing a food allergy is difficult. Humans vomit or have rashes when they eat a food to which they are allergic. Dogs neither vomit nor (usually) develop a rash. They react in the

PROTEIN NEEDS
Your dog's protein needs are changeable. High activity level, stress, climate and other physical factors may require your dog to have more protein in his diet. Check with your breeder about your Westie's needs.

same manner as they do to an airborne or flea allergy: they itch, scratch and bite, thus making the diagnosis extremely difficult. While pollen allergies are usually seasonal, food allergies are year-round problems.

FOOD INTOLERANCE

Food intolerance is the inability of the dog to completely digest certain foods. For instance, puppies that may have done very well on their mother's milk may not do well on cow's milk. The result of this food intolerance may be loose bowels, passing gas and stomach pains. These are the only obvious symptoms of food intolerance, and that makes diagnosis difficult.

TREATING FOOD PROBLEMS

It is possible to handle food allergies and food intolerance yourself. Put your dog on a diet that it has never had. Obviously, if the dog has never eaten this new food, he can't have been allergic or intolerant of it. Start with a single ingredient that is not in the dog's diet at the present time. Ingredients like beef or chicken are common in dog's diets, so try something more exotic like ostrich, rabbit, pheasant or some other protein source. Keep the dog on this diet (with

> **FAT OR FICTION?**
> The myth that dogs need extra fat in their diets can be harmful. Should your vet recommend extra fat, use safflower oil instead of animal oils. Safflower oil has been shown to be less likely to cause allergic reactions.

no additives) for a month. If the symptoms of food allergy or intolerance disappear, chances are your dog has a food allergy.

Don't think that the single ingredient cured the problem. You still must find a suitable diet and ascertain which ingredient in the old diet was objectionable. This is most easily done by adding ingredients to the new diet one at a time. Let the dog stay on the modified diet for a month before you add another ingredient. Eventually, you will determine the ingredient that caused the adverse reaction.

An alternative method is to carefully study the ingredients in the diet to which your dog is allergic or intolerable. Identify the main ingredient in this diet and eliminate the main ingredient by buying a different food that does not have that ingredient. Keep experimenting until the symptoms disappear after one month on the new diet.

A male dog flea, *Ctenocephalides canis.*

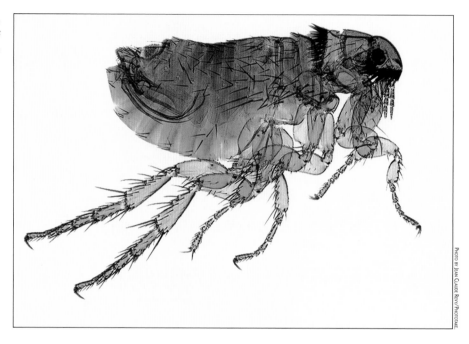

PHOTO BY JEAN CLAUDE REVY/PHOTOTAKE

EXTERNAL PARASITES
FLEAS

Of all the problems to which dogs are prone, none is more well known and frustrating than fleas. Flea infestation is relatively simple to cure but difficult to prevent. Parasites that are harbored inside the body are a bit more difficult to eradicate but they are easier to control.

To control flea infestation, you have to understand the flea's life cycle. Fleas are often thought of as a summertime problem, but centrally heated homes have changed the patterns and fleas can be found at any time of the year. The most effective method of flea control is a two-stage approach: one stage to kill the adult fleas, and the other to control the development of pre-adult fleas. Unfortunately, no single active ingredient is effective against all stages of the life cycle.

FLEA KILLER CAUTION—"POISON"

Flea-killers are poisonous. You should not spray these toxic chemicals on areas of a dog's body that he licks, including his genitals and his face. Flea killers taken internally are a better answer, but check with your vet in case internal therapy is not advised for your dog.

Life Cycle Stages

During its life, a flea will pass through four life stages: egg, larva, pupa or nymph and adult. The adult stage is the most visible and irritating stage of the flea life cycle, and this is why the majority of flea-control products concentrate on this stage. The fact is that adult fleas account for only 1% of the total flea population, and the other 99% exist in pre-adult stages, i.e., eggs, larvae and nymphs. The pre-adult stages are barely visible to the naked eye.

The Life Cycle of the Flea

Eggs are laid on the dog, usually in quantities of about 20 or 30, several times a day. The adult female flea must have a blood meal before each egg-laying session. When first laid, the eggs will cling to the dog's hair, as the eggs are still moist. However, they will quickly dry out and fall from the dog, especially if the dog moves around or scratches. Many eggs will fall off in the dog's favorite area or an area in which he spends a lot of time, such as his bed.

Once the eggs fall from the dog onto the carpet or furniture, they will hatch into larvae. This takes from one to ten days. Larvae are not particularly mobile and will usually travel only a few inches from where they hatch. However, they do have a tendency to move away from bright light and heavy

EN GARDE: CATCHING FLEAS OFF GUARD!
Consider the following ways to arm yourself against fleas:
- Add a small amount of pennyroyal or eucalyptus oil to your dog's bath. These natural remedies repel fleas.
- Supplement your dog's food with fresh garlic (minced or grated) and a hearty amount of brewer's yeast, both of which ward off fleas.
- Use a flea comb on your dog daily. Submerge fleas in a cup of bleach to kill them quickly.
- Confine the dog to only a few rooms to limit the spread of fleas in the home.
- Vacuum daily...and get all of the crevices! Dispose of the bag every few days until the problem is under control.
- Wash your dog's bedding daily. Cover cushions where your dog sleeps with towels, and wash the towels often.

traffic—under furniture and behind doors are common places to find high quantities of flea larvae.

The flea larvae feed on dead organic matter, including adult flea feces, until they are ready to change into adult fleas. Fleas will usually remain as larvae for around seven days. After this period, the larvae will pupate into protective pupae. While inside the pupae, the larvae will undergo metamorphosis and change into

Fleas have been measured as being able to jump 300,000 times and can jump 150 times their length in any direction, including straight up.

adult fleas. This can take as little time as a few days, but the adult fleas can remain inside the pupae waiting to hatch for up to two years. The pupae are signaled to hatch by certain stimuli, such as physical pressure—the pupae's being stepped on, heat from an animal's lying on the pupae or increased carbon-dioxide levels and vibrations—indicating that a suitable host is available.

Once hatched, the adult flea must feed within a few days. Once the adult flea finds a host, it will not leave voluntarily. It only becomes dislodged by grooming or the host animal's scratching. The adult flea will remain on the

PHOTO BY DWIGHT R. KUHN

host for the duration of its life unless forcibly removed.

TREATING THE ENVIRONMENT AND THE DOG

Treating fleas should be a two-pronged attack. First, the environment needs to be treated; this includes carpets and furniture, especially the dog's bedding and areas underneath furniture. The environment should be treated with a household spray containing an Insect Growth Regulator (IGR) and an insecticide to kill the adult fleas. Most IGRs are effective against eggs and larvae; they actually mimic the fleas' own hormones and stop the eggs and larvae from developing into adult fleas. There are currently no treatments available to attack the pupa stage of the life cycle, so the adult insecticide is used to kill the newly hatched adult fleas before they find a host. Most IGRs are active for many months, while adult insecticides are only active

A scanning electron micrograph of a dog or cat flea, *Ctenocephalides*, magnified more than 100x. This image has been colorized for effect.

S. E. M. BY DR DENNIS KUNKEL, UNIVERSITY OF HAWAII

THE LIFE CYCLE OF THE FLEA

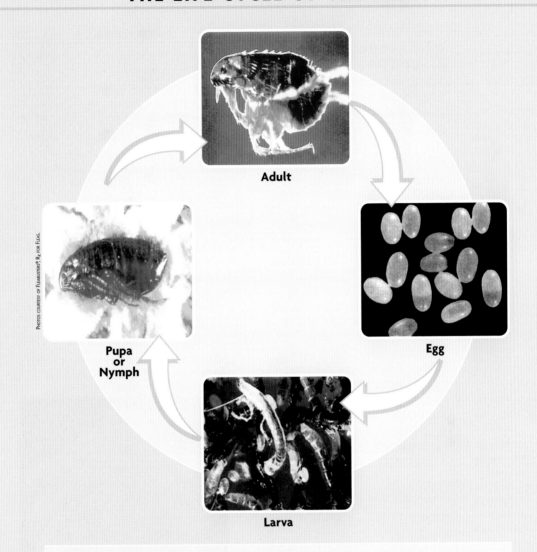

Adult

Egg

Larva

Pupa
or
Nymph

PHOTOS COURTESY OF FLEABUSTERS® RX FOR FLEAS.

Fleas have been around for millions of years and have adapted to changing host animals. They are able to go through a complete life cycle in less than one month or they can extend their lives to almost two years by remaining as pupae or cocoons. They do not need blood or any other food for up to 20 months.

INSECT GROWTH REGULATOR (IGR)

Two types of products should be used when treating fleas—a product to treat the pet and a product to treat the home. Adult fleas represent less than 1% of the flea population. The pre-adult fleas (eggs, larvae and pupae) represent more than 99% of the flea population and are found in the environment; it is in the case of pre-adult fleas that products containing an Insect Growth Regulator (IGR) should be used in the home.

IGRs are a new class of compounds used to prevent the development of insects. They do not kill the insect outright, but instead use the insect's biology against it to stop it from completing its growth. Products that contain methoprene are the world's first and leading IGRs. Used to control fleas and other insects, this type of IGR will stop flea larvae from developing and protect the house for up to seven months.

The American dog tick, Dermacentor variabilis, is probably the most common tick found on dogs. Look at the strength in its eight legs! No wonder it's hard to detach them.

is to apply an adult insecticide to the dog. Traditionally, this would be in the form of a collar or a spray, but more recent innovations include digestible insecticides that poison the fleas when they ingest the dog's blood. Alternatively, there are drops that, when placed on the back of the dog's neck, spread throughout the hair and skin to kill adult fleas.

TICKS

Though not as common as fleas, ticks are found all over the tropical and temperate world. They don't bite, like fleas; they harpoon. They dig their sharp proboscis (nose) into the dog's skin and drink the blood. Their only food and drink is dog's

for a few days.

When treating with a household spray, it is a good idea to vacuum before applying the product. This stimulates as many pupae as possible to hatch into adult fleas. The vacuum cleaner should also be treated with an insecticide to prevent the eggs and larvae that have been collected in the vacuum bag from hatching.

The second stage of treatment

S. E. M. by Dr. Dennis Kunkel, University of Hawaii

blood. Dogs can get Lyme disease, Rocky Mountain spotted fever, tick bite paralysis and many other diseases from ticks. They may live where fleas are found and they like to hide in cracks or seams in walls. They are controlled the same way fleas are controlled.

The American dog tick, *Dermacentor variabilis*, may well be the most common dog tick in many geographical areas, especially those areas where the climate is hot and humid. Most dog ticks have life expectancies of a week to six months, depending upon climatic conditions. They can neither jump nor fly, but they can crawl slowly and can range up to 16 feet to reach a sleeping or unsuspecting dog.

Mites

Just as fleas and ticks can be problematic for your dog, mites can also lead to an itchy nuisance. Microscopic in size, mites are related to ticks and generally take up permanent residence on their host animal— in this case, your dog! The term *mange* refers to any infestation caused by one of the mighty mites, of which there are six varieties that concern dog owners.

Demodex mites cause a condition known as demodicosis (sometimes called red mange or

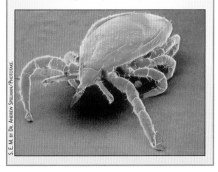

DEER-TICK CROSSING

The great outdoors may be fun for your dog, but it also is a home to dangerous ticks. Deer ticks carry a bacterium known as *Borrelia burgdorferi* and are most active in the autumn and spring. When infections are caught early, penicillin and tetracycline are effective antibiotics, but if left untreated the bacteria may cause neurological, kidney and cardiac problems as well as long-term trouble with walking and painful joints.

S.E.M. BY DR. ANDREW SPIELMAN/PHOTOTAKE.

PHOTO BY DR. DENNIS KUNKEL, UNIVERSITY OF HAWAII.

The head of an American dog tick, *Dermacentor variabilis*, enlarged and colorized for effect.

The mange mite, *Psoroptes bovis*, can infest cattle and other domestic animals.

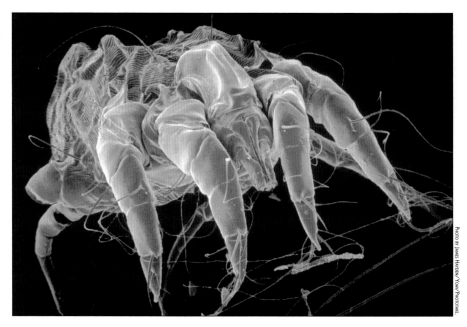

PHOTO BY JAMES HAYDEN/YOAV/PHOTOTAKE.

follicular mange), in which the mites live in the dog's hair follicles and sebaceous glands in larger-than-normal numbers. This type of mange is commonly passed from the dam to her puppies and usually shows up on the puppies' muzzles, though demodicosis is not transferable from one normal dog to another. Most dogs recover from this type of mange without any treatment, though topical therapies are commonly prescribed by the vet.

Human lice look like dog lice; the two are closely related.

PHOTO BY DWIGHT R. KUHN.

The *Cheyletiellosis* mite is the hook-mouthed culprit associated with "walking dandruff," a condition that affects dogs as well as cats and rabbits. This mite lives on the surface of the animal's skin and is readily transferable through direct or indirect contact with an affected animal. The dandruff is present in the form of scaly skin, which may or may not be itchy. If not treated, this mange can affect a whole kennel of dogs and can be spread to humans as well.

The *Sarcoptes* mite causes intense itching on the dog in the form of a condition known as scabies or sarcoptic mange. The cycle of the *Sarcoptes* mite lasts about three weeks, and the mites live in the top layer of the dog's skin (epidermis), preferably in areas with little hair. Scabies is highly contagious and can be passed to humans. Sometimes an allergic reaction to the mite worsens the severe itching associated with sarcoptic mange.

Ear mites, *Otodectes cynotis,* lead to otodectic mange, which most commonly affects the outer ear canal of the dog, though other areas can be affected as well. Dogs with ear-mite infestation commonly scratch at their ears, causing further irritation, and shake their heads. Dark brown droppings in the outer ear confirm the diagnosis. Your vet can prescribe a treatment to flush out the ears and kill any eggs in the ears. A complete month of treatment is necessary to cure the mange.

Two other mites, less common in dogs, include *Dermanyssus gallinae* (the poultry or red mite) and *Eutrombicula alfreddugesi* (the North American mite associated with trombiculidiasis or chigger infestation). The poultry mite frequently lives on chickens, but can transfer to dogs who spend time near farm animals. Chigger infestation affects dogs in the

NOT A DROP TO DRINK
Never allow your dog to swim in polluted water or public areas where water quality can be suspect. Even perfectly clear water can harbor parasites, many of which can cause serious to fatal illnesses in canines. Areas inhabited by waterfowl and other wildlife are especially dangerous.

Central U.S. who have exposure to woodlands. The types of mange caused by both of these mites are treatable by vets.

INTERNAL PARASITES

Most animals—fishes, birds and mammals, including dogs and humans—have worms and other parasites that live inside their bodies. According to Dr. Herbert R. Axelrod, the fish pathologist, there are two kinds of parasites: dumb and smart. The smart parasites live in peaceful cooperation with their hosts (symbiosis), while the dumb parasites kill their hosts. Most worm infections are relatively easy to control. If they are not controlled, they weaken the host dog to the point that other medical problems occur, but they do not kill the host as dumb parasites would.

A brown dog tick, *Rhipicephalus sanguineus*, is an uncommon but annoying tick found on dogs.

PHOTO BY CAROLINA BIOLOGICAL SUPPLY/PHOTOTAKE.

DO NOT MIX
Never mix parasite-control products without first consulting your vet. Some products can become toxic when combined with others and can cause fatal consequences.

The roundworm *Rhabditis* can infect both dogs and humans.

ROUNDWORMS

Average-size dogs can pass 1,360,000 roundworm eggs every day. For example, if there were only 1 million dogs in the world, the world would be saturated with thousands of tons of dog feces. These feces would contain around 15,000,000,000 roundworm eggs.

Up to 31% of home yards and children's sand boxes in the U.S. contain roundworm eggs.

Flushing dog's feces down the toilet is not a safe practice because the usual sewage treatments do not destroy roundworm eggs.

Infected puppies start shedding roundworm eggs at three weeks of age. They can be infected by their mother's milk.

The roundworm, *Ascaris lumbricoides.*

ROUNDWORMS

The roundworms that infect dogs are known scientifically as *Toxocara canis*. They live in the dog's intestines and shed eggs continually. It has been estimated that a dog produces about 6 or more ounces of feces every day. Each ounce of feces averages hundreds of thousands of roundworm eggs. There are no known areas in which dogs roam that do not contain roundworm eggs. The greatest danger of roundworms is that they infect people, too! It is wise to have your dog tested regularly for roundworms.

In young puppies, roundworms cause bloated bellies, diarrhea, coughing and vomiting, and are transmitted from the dam (through blood or milk). Affected puppies will not appear as animated as normal puppies. The worms appear spaghetti-like, measuring as long as 6 inches. Adult dogs can acquire roundworms through coprophagia (eating contaminated feces) or by killing rodents that carry roundworms.

Roundworm infection can kill puppies and cause severe problems in adults, as the hatched larvae travel to the lungs and trachea through the bloodstream. Cleanliness is the best preventative for roundworms. Always pick up after your dog and dispose of feces in appropriate receptacles.

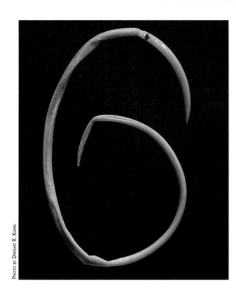

PHOTO BY DWIGHT R. KUHN.

HOOKWORMS

In the United States, dog owners have to be concerned about four different species of hookworm, the most common and most serious of which is *Ancylostoma caninum,* which prefers warm climates. The others are *Ancylostoma braziliense, Ancylostoma tubaeforme* and *Uncinaria stenocephala,* the latter of which is a concern to dogs living in the Northern U.S. and Canada, as this species prefers cold climates. Hookworms are dangerous to humans as well as to dogs and cats, and can be the cause of severe anemia due to iron deficiency. The worm uses its teeth to attach itself to the dog's intestines and changes the site of its attachment about six times per day. Each time the worm repositions itself, the dog loses blood and can become anemic. *Ancylostoma caninum* is the most likely of the four species to cause anemia in the dog.

Symptoms of hookworm infection include dark stools, weight loss, general weakness, pale coloration and anemia, as well as possible skin problems. Fortunately, hookworms are easily purged from the affected dog with a number of medications that have proven effective. Discuss these with your vet. Most heartworm preventatives include a hookworm insecticide as well.

Owners also must be aware that hookworms can infect humans, who can acquire the larvae through exposure to contaminated feces. Since the worms cannot complete their life cycle on a human, the worms simply infest the skin and cause irritation. This condition is known as cutaneous larva migrans syndrome. As a preventative, use disposable gloves or a "poop-scoop" to pick up your dog's droppings and prevent your dog (or neighborhood cats) from defecating in children's play areas.

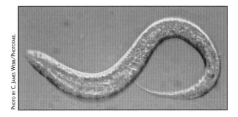

PHOTO BY C. JAMES WEBB/PHOTOTAKE.

The infective stage of the hookworm larva.

TAPEWORMS

Humans, rats, squirrels, foxes, coyotes, wolves and domestic dogs are all susceptible to tapeworm infection. Except in humans, tapeworms are usually not a fatal infection. Infected individuals can harbor 1000 parasitic worms.

Tapeworms, like some other types of worm, are hermaphroditic, meaning male and female in the same worm.

If dogs eat infected rats or mice, or anything else infected with tapeworm, they get the tapeworm disease. One month after attaching to a dog's intestine, the worm starts shedding eggs. These eggs are infective immediately. Infective eggs can live for a few months without a host animal.

The head and rostellum (the round prominence on the scolex) of a tapeworm, which infects dogs and humans.

PHOTO BY CAROLINA BIOLOGICAL SUPPLY/PHOTOTAKE.

TAPEWORMS

There are many species of tapeworm, all of which are carried by fleas! The most common tapeworm affecting dogs is known as *Dipylidium caninum*. The dog eats the flea and starts the tapeworm cycle. Humans can also be infected with tapeworms—so don't eat fleas! Fleas are so small that your dog could pass them onto your hands, your plate or your food and thus make it possible for you to ingest a flea that is carrying tapeworm eggs.

While tapeworm infection is not life-threatening in dogs (smart parasite!), it can be the cause of a very serious liver disease for humans. About 50% of the humans infected with *Echinococcus multilocularis*, a type of tapeworm that causes alveolar hydatid, perish.

WHIPWORMS

In North America, whipworms are counted among the most common parasitic worms in dogs. The whipworm's scientific name is *Trichuris vulpis*. These worms attach themselves in the lower parts of the intestine, where they feed. Affected dogs may only experience upset tummies, colic and diarrhea. These worms, however, can live for months or years in the dog, beginning their larval stage in the small intestine, spending their adult stage in the large intestine and finally passing infective eggs through the dog's feces. The only way to detect whipworms is through a fecal examination, though this is not always foolproof. Treatment for whipworms is tricky, due to the worms' unusual life-cycle pattern, and very often dogs are reinfected due to exposure to infective eggs on the ground. The whipworm eggs can survive in the environment for as long as five years; thus, cleaning up droppings in your own backyard as well as in public places is absolutely essential for sanitation purposes and the health of your dog and others.

THREADWORMS

Though less common than roundworms, hookworms and those previously mentioned, threadworms concern dog owners in the Southwestern U.S. and Gulf Coast area where the climate is hot and humid. Living in the small intestine of the dog, this worm measures a mere 2 millimeters and is round in shape. Like that of the whipworm, the threadworm's life cycle is very complex and the eggs and larvae are passed through the feces. A deadly disease in humans, *Strongyloides* readily infects people, and the handling of feces is the most common means of transmission. Threadworms are most often seen in young puppies; bloody diarrhea and pneumonia are symptoms. Sick puppies must be isolated and treated immediately; vets recommend a follow-up treatment one month later.

HEARTWORM PREVENTATIVES

There are many heartworm preventatives on the market, many of which are sold at your veterinarian's office. These products can be given daily or monthly, depending on the manufacturer's instructions. All of these preventatives contain chemical insecticides directed at killing heartworms, which leads to some controversy among dog owners. In effect, heartworm preventatives are necessary evils, though you should determine how necessary based on your pet's lifestyle. There is no doubt that heartworm is a dreadful disease that threatens the lives of dogs. However, the likelihood of your dog's being bitten by an infected mosquito is slim in most places, and a mosquito-repellent (or an herbal remedy such as Wormwood or Black Walnut) is much safer for your dog and will not compromise his immune system (the way heartworm preventatives will). Should you decide to use the traditional preventative "medications," you can consider giving the pill every other or third month. Since the toxins in the pill will kill the heartworms at all stages of development, the pill would be effective in killing larvae, nymphs or adults and it takes four months for the larvae to reach the adult stage. Thus, there is no rationale to poisoning the dog's system on a monthly basis. Lastly, do not give the pill during the winter months since there are no mosquitoes around to pass on their infection, unless you live in a tropical environment.

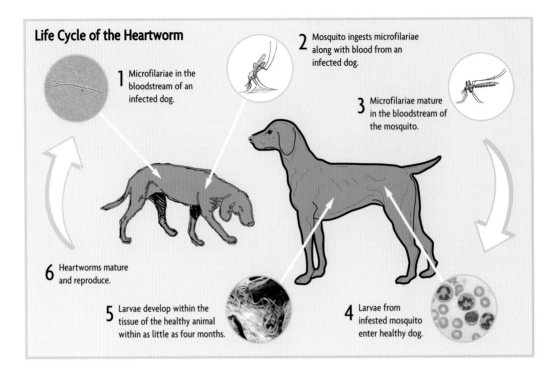

Life Cycle of the Heartworm

1 Microfilariae in the bloodstream of an infected dog.

2 Mosquito ingests microfilariae along with blood from an infected dog.

3 Microfilariae mature in the bloodstream of the mosquito.

4 Larvae from infested mosquito enter healthy dog.

5 Larvae develop within the tissue of the healthy animal within as little as four months.

6 Heartworms mature and reproduce.

HEARTWORMS

Heartworms are thin, extended worms up to 12 inches long, which live in a dog's heart and the major blood vessels surrounding it. Dogs may have up to 200 worms. Symptoms may be loss of energy, loss of appetite, coughing, the development of a pot belly and anemia.

Heartworms are transmitted by mosquitoes. The mosquito drinks the blood of an infected dog and takes in larvae with the blood. The larvae, called microfilariae, develop within the body of the mosquito and are passed on to the next dog bitten after the larvae mature. It takes two to three weeks for the larvae to develop to the infective stage within the body of the mosquito. Dogs are usually treated at about six weeks of age and maintained on a prophylactic dose given monthly.

Blood testing for heartworms is not necessarily indicative of how seriously your dog is infected. Although this is a dangerous disease, it is not easy for a dog to be infected. Discuss the various preventatives with your vet, as there are many different types now available. Together you can decide on a safe course of prevention for your dog.

Magnified heartworm larvae, *Dirofilaria immitis.*

PHOTO BY CAROLINA BIOLOGICAL SUPPLY/PHOTOTAKE.

Heartworm, *Dirofilaria immitis.*

PHOTO BY J E HAYDEN, RBP/PHOTOTAKE.

The heart of a dog infected with canine heartworm, *Dirofilaria immitis.*

PHOTO BY JAMIE E. HAYDEN, RPB/PHOTOTAKE.

HEALTH PROBLEMS
MOST FREQUENTLY SEEN IN WEST HIGHLAND WHITE TERRIERS

Condition	Age Affected	Cause	Area Affected
Aortic Stenosis	Young pups	Congenital	Heart
Cataracts (cloudiness on lens)	Before 1 year	Congenital	Eyes
Copper Toxicosis	Adults	Congenital	Liver
Craniomandibular Osteopathy	4 to 7 mos	Congenital	Bones of lower jaw, inner ear, head
Elbow Dysplasia	4 to 7 mos	Congenital	Elbow joint (forequarter lameness)
Epidermal Dysplasia	Young pups	Congenital	Skin
Gastric Dilatation (Bloat)	Older dogs	Swallowing air	Stomach
Globoid Cell Leukodystrophy	11 to 30 weeks	Congenital	Neurological
Hip Dysplasia	By 2 years	Congenital	Hip joint
Hypothyroidism	1 to 3 years	Congenital	Endocrine system
Inhalant Allergies	After 6 months	Atmospheric	Skin reactions
Keratoconjunctivitis Sicca	Any age	Drug reactions	Eyes
Legg-Calve-Perthes Disease	4 to 10 months	Injury/diet	Leg (hindquarter lameness)
Liver Disease	2 to 4 years	Congenital	Liver
Medical Patellar Luxation	Any age	Poss. congenital	Slipped kneecap
Osteochondrosis	4 to 7 months	Congenital	Cartilage (forequarter lameness)
Primary Glaucoma	Over 5 years	Hereditary	Eyes (blindness)
Von Willebrand's Disease	Birth	Congenital	Blood

WEST HIGHLAND WHITE TERRIER

The term *old* is a qualitative term. For dogs, as well as their masters, old is relative. Certainly we can all distinguish between a puppy West Highland White Terrier and an adult West Highland White Terrier—there

are the obvious physical traits, such as size, appearance and facial expressions, and personality traits. Puppies and young dogs like to play with children. Children's natural exuberance is a good match for the seemingly endless energy of young dogs. They like to run, jump, chase and retrieve. When dogs grow up and cease their interaction with children, they are often thought of as being too old to play with the kids.

On the other hand, if a West Highland White Terrier is only exposed to people with quieter lifestyles, his life will normally be less active and the age-related changes in his activity level will not be as noticeable.

If people live to be 100 years old, dogs live to be 20 years old. While this may seem like a good rule of thumb, it is very inaccurate. When trying to compare dog years to human years, you cannot make a generalization about all dogs. Terriers as a whole are long-lived dogs and your Westie will be no different. If your Westie lives to be eight years of age, you can be

As your Westie gets older, his physical and mental abilities diminish. He deserves special attention from his owner during his golden years.

GETTING OLD
The bottom line is simply that a dog is getting old when you think he is getting old because he slows down in his general activities, including walking, running, eating, jumping and retrieving. On the other hand, certain activities increase, like more sleeping, more barking and more repetition of habits like going to the door when you put your coat on without being called.

SIGNS OF AGING

An old dog starts to show one or more of the following symptoms:

- Sleep patterns are deeper and longer and the old dog is harder to awaken.

- Food intake diminishes.

- Responses to calls, whistles and other signals are ignored more and more.

- Eye contacts do not evoke tail wagging (assuming they once did).

- The hair on its face and paws starts to turn gray. The color breakdown usually starts around the eyes and mouth.

Opposite page: There is no fixed rule about how a Westie will act at any given age. Think about your human friends and how they change as time goes on.

pretty certain that he will last until 12 or more years of age. I have friends who had four Westies that lived to be 14 to 16 years of age. Indeed, 16 years is a long time for a little white dog to live!

Dogs are generally considered mature within three years, but they can reproduce even earlier. So the first three years of a dog's life are like seven times that of comparable humans. That means a 3-year-old dog is like a 21-year-old human. As the curve of comparison shows, though, there is no hard and fast rule for comparing dog and human ages. The comparison is made even more difficult, for not all

humans age at the same rate...and human females live longer than human males.

WHAT TO LOOK FOR IN SENIORS

Most veterinarians and behaviorists use the seven-year mark as the time to consider a dog a "senior." The term "senior" does not imply that the dog is geriatric and has begun to fail in mind and body. Aging is essentially a slowing process. Humans readily admit that they feel a difference in their activity level from age 20 to 30, and then from 30 to 40, etc. By treating the seven-year-old dog as a senior, owners are able to implement certain therapeutic

SENIOR APPETITES

Your senior dog may lose interest in eating, not because he's less hungry but because his senses of smell and taste have diminished. The old chow simply does not smell as good as it once did. Additionally, older dogs use less energy and thereby can sustain themselves on less food.

and preventative medical strategies with the help of their veterinarians. A senior-care program should include at least two veterinary visits per year and screening sessions to determine the dog's health status, as well as

Sometimes older Westies become confused and less social. These are the times that your Westie needs additional reassurance.

nutritional counseling. Veterinarians can determine the senior dog's health status through a blood smear for a complete blood count, serum chemistry profile with electrolytes, urinalysis, blood pressure check, electrocardiogram, ocular tonometry (pressure on the eyeball), and dental prophylaxis.

Such an extensive program for senior dogs is well advised before owners start to see the obvious physical signs of aging, such as slower and inhibited movement, graying, increased sleep/nap periods and disinterest in play and other activity. This preventative program promises a longer, healthier life for the aging dog. Among the physical problems common in aging dogs are the loss of sight and hearing, arthritis, kidney and liver failure, diabetes mellitus, heart disease and Cushing's disease (a hormonal disease).

In addition to the physical manifestations discussed, there are some behavioral changes and problems related to aging dogs.

Dogs suffering from hearing or vision loss, dental discomfort or arthritis can become aggressive. Likewise, the near-deaf and/or blind dog may be startled more easily and react in an unexpectedly aggressive manner. Seniors suffering from senility can become more impatient and irritable. Housesoiling accidents are associated with loss of mobility, kidney problems and loss of sphincter control as well as plaque accumulation, physiological brain

Senior dogs will not be able to perform many of the tasks and antics they enjoyed in their youth.

NOTICING THE SYMPTOMS

The symptoms listed below are symptoms that gradually appear and become more noticeable. They are not life-threatening; however, the symptoms below are to be taken very seriously and warrant a discussion with your veterinarian:

• Your dog cries and whimpers when he moves, and he stops running completely.

• Convulsions start or become more serious and frequent. The usual convulsion (spasm) is when the dog stiffens and starts to tremble, being unable or unwilling to move. The seizure usually lasts for 5 to 30 minutes.

• Your dog drinks more water and urinates more frequently. Wetting and bowel accidents take place indoors without warning.

• Vomiting becomes more and more frequent.

Your dog's body temperature is a good start to ascertaining the general health of your Westie. Learn how to do this yourself.

changes and reactions to medications. Older dogs, just like young puppies, suffer from separation anxiety, which can lead to excessive barking, whining, housesoiling and destructive behavior. Seniors may become fearful of everyday sounds, such as vacuum cleaners, heaters, thunder and passing traffic. Some dogs have difficulty sleeping, due to discomfort, the need for frequent potty visits and the like.

Owners should avoid spoiling the older dog with too many fatty treats. Obesity is a common problem in older dogs and subtracts years from their lives. Keep the senior dog as trim as possible since excessive weight puts additional stress on the body's vital organs. Some breeders recommend supplementing the diet with foods high in fiber and lower in calories.

Adding fresh vegetables and marrow broth to the senior's diet makes a tasty, low-calorie, low-fat supplement. Vets also offer specialty diets for senior dogs that are worth exploring.

Your dog, as he nears his twilight years, needs his owner's patience and good care more than ever. Never punish an older dog for an accident or abnormal behavior. For all the years of love, protection and companionship that your dog has provided, he deserves special attention and courtesies. The older dog may need to relieve himself at 3 a.m. because he can no longer hold it for eight hours. Older dogs may not be able to remain crated for more than two or three hours. It may be time to give up a sofa or chair to your old friend. Although he may not seem as enthusiastic about your attention and petting, he does appreciate the considerations you offer as he gets older.

Your West Highland White Terrier does not understand why his world is slowing down. Owners must make the transition into the golden years as pleasant and rewarding as possible.

WHAT TO DO WHEN THE TIME COMES

You are never fully prepared to make a rational decision about putting your dog to sleep. It is very obvious that you love your

CDS: COGNITIVE DYSFUNCTION SYNDROME
"Old-Dog Syndrome"

There are many ways for you to evaluate old-dog syndrome. Veterinarians have defined CDS (cognitive dysfunction syndrome) as the gradual deterioration of cognitive abilities. These are indicated by changes in the dog's behavior. When a dog changes his routine response, and maladies have been eliminated as the cause of these behavioral changes, then CDS is the usual diagnosis.

More than half the dogs over eight years old suffer from some form of CDS. The older the dog, the more chance he has of suffering from CDS. In humans, doctors often dismiss the CDS behavioral changes as part of "winding down."

There are four major signs of CDS: frequent potty accidents inside the home, sleeping much more or much less than normal, acting confused and failing to respond to social stimuli.

SYMPTOMS OF CDS

FREQUENT POTTY ACCIDENTS
- *Urinates in the house.*
- *Defecates in the house.*
- *Doesn't signal that he wants to go out.*

SLEEP PATTERNS
- *Awakens more slowly.*
- *Sleeps more than normal during the day.*
- *Sleeps less during the night.*

CONFUSION
- *Goes outside and just stands there.*
- *Appears confused with a faraway look in his eyes.*
- *Hides more often.*
- *Doesn't recognize friends.*
- *Doesn't come when called.*
- *Walks around listlessly and without a destination.*

FAILURE TO RESPOND TO SOCIAL STIMULI
- *Comes to people less frequently, whether called or not.*
- *Doesn't tolerate petting for more than a short time.*
- *Doesn't come to the door when you return home.*

West Highland White Terrier or you would not be reading this book. Putting a loved dog to sleep is extremely difficult. It is a decision that must be made with your veterinarian. You are usually forced to make the decision when one of the life-threatening symptoms listed previously becomes serious enough for you to seek veterinary help for your dog.

If the prognosis of the malady indicates the end is near and your beloved pet will only suffer more and experience no enjoyment for the balance of his life, then euthanasia is the right choice.

TALK IT OUT
The more open discussion you have about the whole stressful occurrence, the easier it will be for you when the time comes. There are online services, chat groups and many excellent books for you to explore.

WHAT IS EUTHANASIA?
Euthanasia derives from the Greek, meaning *good death*. In other words, it means the planned, painless killing of a dog suffering from a painful, incurable condition, or who is so aged that cannot walk, see, eat or control his excretory functions.
Euthanasia is usually

Consult your vet to help you locate a nice pet cemetery near your home.

Pet owners can choose to memorialize their deceased canine friends with special markers.

accomplished by injection with an overdose of an anesthesia or barbiturate. Aside from the prick of the needle, the experience is usually painless.

The decision to euthanize your dog is never easy. The days during which the dog becomes ill and the end occurs can be unusually stressful for you. If this is your first experience with the death of a loved one, you may need the comfort dictated by your religious beliefs. If you are the head of the family and have children, you should have involved them in the decision of putting your West Highland White Terrier to sleep. Usually your dog can be maintained on drugs for a few days while he is kept in the clinic in order to give you ample time to make a decision. During this time, talking with members of the family and people who have lived through this same experience can ease the burden of your inevitable decision. In any case, euthanasia can be very stressful for the family of the dog.

THE FINAL RESTING PLACE
Dogs can have the same privileges as humans. A dog can

EUTHANASIA SERVICES
Euthanasia must be done by a licensed vet, who may be considerate enough to come to your home. There also may be societies for the prevention of cruelty to animals in your area. They often offer this service upon a vet's recommendation.

Some pet cemeteries have inexpensive sites in which you can store your deceased pet's ashes.

be buried in a pet cemetery in a burial container; buried in your yard in a place suitably marked with a stone, newly planted tree or bush; or cremated, with the ashes being given to you.

All of these options should be discussed frankly and openly with your veterinarian. Do not be afraid to ask financial questions. The less costly cremations are mass burnings, but your dog's ashes cannot be returned. If you want a private cremation, there are small crematoriums available to all veterinary clinics. Your vet can usually arrange this, but it is more expensive.

GETTING ANOTHER DOG?
The grief of losing your beloved dog will be as lasting as the grief of losing a human friend or relative. In most cases, if your dog died of old age (if there is such a thing), it

had slowed down considerably. Do you want a new West Highland White Terrier puppy to replace it? Or are you better off finding a more mature West Highland White Terrier, say two to three years of age, which will usually be housetrained and will have an already developed personality. In this case, you can find out if you like each other after a few hours of being together.

The decision is, of course, your own. Do you want another West Highland White Terrier? Perhaps you want a smaller or larger dog? Look in your local newspapers for advertisements, or, better yet, consult your local society for the prevention of cruelty to animals to adopt a dog. It is harder to find puppies at an animal shelter, but there are often many adult dogs in need of good homes. You may be able to find another West Highland White Terrier, or you may choose another breed or a mixed-breed dog.

Private breeders, of course, are the best source for high-quality puppies and dogs. You may be able to "rescue" an abandoned Westie or to purchase a retired show dog from a breeder. Both of these options are excellent ways to resume your membership in the Westie fraternity.

WEST HIGHLAND WHITE TERRIER

As a West Highland White Terrier owner, you have selected your dog so that you and your loved ones can have a companion, a rodent exterminator, a friend and a four-legged family member. You invest time, money and effort to care for and train the family's new charge. Of course, this chosen canine behaves perfectly! Well, perfectly like a *dog*.

THINK LIKE A DOG

Dogs do not think like humans, nor do humans think like dogs, though we try. Unfortunately, a dog is incapable of figuring out how humans think, so the responsibility falls on the owner to adopt a proper canine mindset. Dogs cannot rationalize, and dogs exist in the present moment. Many a dog owner makes the mistake in training of thinking that he can reprimand his dog for something he did a while ago. Basically, you cannot even reprimand a dog for something he did 20 seconds ago! Either catch him in the act or forget it! It is a waste of both your time and your dog's time—in his mind, you are reprimanding him for whatever he is doing at that moment.

The following behavioral problems represent some which owners most commonly encounter. Every dog is unique and every situation is unique. No author could purport for you to solve your West Highland White Terrier's problem simply by reading a script. Here we outline some basic "dogspeak" so that owners' chances of solving behavioral problems are increased. Discuss bad habits with your veterinarian and he/she can recommend a behavioral specialist to consult in appropriate cases. Since behavioral abnormalities are the leading reason that owners

CANDID CAMERA
Dogs and humans may be the only animals that *smile*. Dogs imitate the smile on their owner's face when he greets a friend. The dog only smiles at its human friends. It never smiles at another dog or cat. Usually it rolls up its lips and shows its teeth in a clenched mouth while it rolls over onto its back, begging for a soft scratch.

> **EXPLOSIVE GIFT**
> Dog aggression is a serious problem. *Never* give an aggressive dog to someone else without giving the new owners a complete profile of the dog's behavior problems. The dog will usually be more aggressive in a new situation where his leadership is unchallenged and unquestioned (in his mind).

abandon their pets, we hope that you will make a valiant effort to solve your West Highland White Terrier's problems. Patience and understanding are virtues that must dwell in every pet-loving household.

AGGRESSION

This is a problem that concerns some owners of West Highland White Terriers. Aggression can be a very big problem in dogs, especially in terriers that do not readily accept other canines. Aggression, when not controlled, always becomes dangerous. An aggressive dog, no matter the size, may lunge at, bite or even attack a person or another dog. Aggressive behavior is not to be tolerated. It is painful for a family to watch their dog become unpredictable in his behavior to the point where they are afraid of him. While not all aggressive behavior is dangerous, growling, baring teeth, etc., can be frightening. It is

important to ascertain why the dog is acting in this manner. Aggression is a display of dominance, and the dog should not have the dominant role in his pack, which is, in this case, your family.

It is important not to challenge an aggressive dog as this could provoke an attack. Observe your West Highland White Terrier's body language. Does he make direct eye contact and stare? Does he try to make himself as large as possible: ears pricked, chest out, tail erect? Height and size signify authority in a dog pack—being taller or "above" another dog literally means that he is "above" in the social status. These body signals tell you that your West Highland White Terrier thinks he is in charge, a problem that needs to be addressed. An aggressive dog is unpredictable: you never know when he is going to strike and what he is going to do. You cannot understand why a dog that is playful and loving one minute is growling and snapping the next.

Fear is a common cause of aggression in dogs. If you can isolate what brings out the fear reaction, you can help the dog get over it. Supervise your West Highland White Terrier's interactions with people and other dogs, and praise the dog when it goes well. If he starts to act aggres-

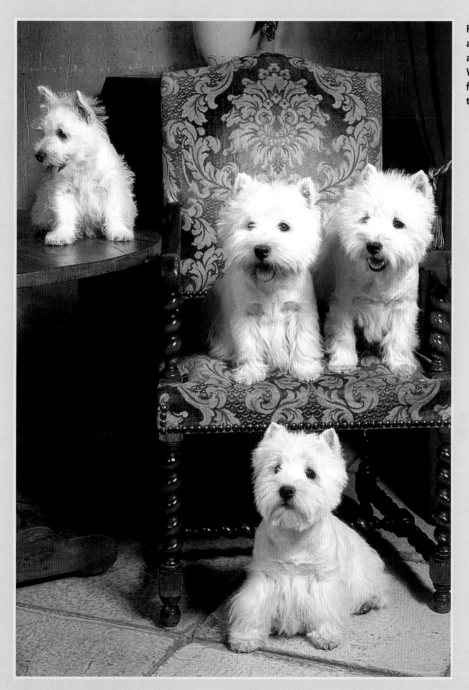

Few things are as rewarding as a family of Westies, beautifully captured in this portrait.

Well-socialized puppies, which have proper introductions to other dogs, will grow up to be more accepting of other canines.

sively in a situation, correct him and remove him from the situation. Do not let people approach the dog and start petting him without your express permission. That way, you can have the dog sit to accept petting and praise him when he behaves properly. You are focusing on praise and on modifying his behavior by rewarding him when he acts appropriately. By being gentle and by supervising his interactions, you are showing him that there is no need to be afraid or defensive.

The best solution is to consult a behavioral specialist, one who has experience with the West Highland White Terrier, if possible. Together, perhaps you can pinpoint the cause of your dog's aggression and do something about it. An aggressive dog cannot be trusted, and a dog that cannot be trusted is not safe to have as a family pet. If the pet Westie becomes untrustworthy, he cannot be kept in the home with the family. The family must get rid of

the dog. In the worst case, the dog must be euthanized.

AGGRESSION TOWARD OTHER DOGS
In general, a dog's aggressive behavior toward another dog stems from not enough exposure to other dogs at an early age. In West Highland White Terriers, early socialization with other dogs is absolutely essential since most terriers are feisty around other dogs. If other dogs make your West Highland White Terrier nervous and agitated, he will lash out as a defensive mechanism. A dog who has not received sufficient exposure to other canines tends to believe that he is the only dog on the planet. The animal becomes so dominant that he does not even show signs that he is fearful or threatened. Without growling or any other physical signal as a warning, he will lunge at and bite the other dog. A way to correct this is to let your West Highland White Terrier

ACT COOL

If you are approached by an aggressive, growling dog, do not run away. Simply stand still, act casual and avoid eye contact. If you have something in your hand (like a handbag), throw it sideways away from your body to distract the dog from making a frontal attack. Dogs sense fear and will act accordingly.

FEAR FACTOR

Fear in a grown dog is often the result of improper or incomplete socialization as a pup, or it can be the result of a traumatic experience he suffered when young. Keep in mind that the term "traumatic" is relative—something that you would not think twice about can leave a lasting negative impression on a puppy. If the dog experiences a similar experience later in life, he may try to fight back to protect himself. Again, this behavior is very unpredictable, especially if you do not know what is triggering his fear.

under him and please those above him. Dogs know that there must be a leader. If you are not the obvious choice for emperor, the dog will assume the throne! These conflicting innate desires are what a dog owner is up against when he sets about training a dog. In training a dog to obey commands, the owner is reinforcing that he is the top dog in the "pack" and that the dog should, and should want to, serve his superior. Thus, the owner is suppressing the dog's urge to dominate by modifying his behavior and making him obedient.

An important part of training is taking every opportunity to reinforce that you are the leader. The simple action of making your

A well-bred and well-socialized Westie puppy will not exhibit any unusual aggressive behavior. Owners must learn to recognize normal canine behavior, such as play biting and the like.

approach another dog when walking on lead. Watch very closely and at the very first sign of aggression, correct your West Highland White Terrier and pull him away. Scold him for any sign of discomfort and then praise him when he ignores or tolerates the other dog. Keep this up until he stops the aggressive behavior, learns to ignore the other dog or accepts other dogs. Praise him lavishly for his correct behavior.

DOMINANT AGGRESSION

A social hierarchy is firmly established in a wild dog pack. The dog wants to dominate those

West Highland White Terrier sit to wait for his food says that you control when he eats and that he is dependent on you for food. Although it may be difficult, do not give in to your dog's wishes every time he whines at you or looks at you with his pleading eyes. It is a constant effort to show the dog that his place in the pack is at the bottom. This is not meant to sound cruel or inhumane. You love your Westie and you should treat him with care and affection. You (hopefully) did not get a dog just so you could control another creature. Dog training is not about being cruel or feeling important, it is about molding the dog's behavior into what is acceptable and teaching him to live by your rules. In theory, it is quite simple: catch him in appropriate behavior and reward him for it. Add a dog into the equation and it becomes a bit more trying, but, as a rule of thumb, positive reinforcement is what works best.

With a dominant dog, punishment and negative reinforcement can have the opposite effect of what you are after. It can make a dog fearful and/or act out aggressively if he feels he is being challenged. Remember, a dominant dog perceives himself at the top of the social heap and will fight to defend his perceived status. The best way to prevent that is never to give him reason to think that he is in control in the first place. If you are having trouble training your West Highland White Terrier and it seems as if he is constantly challenging your authority, seek the help of an obedience trainer or behavioral specialist. A professional will work with both you and your dog to teach you effective techniques to use at home. Beware of trainers who rely on excessively harsh methods;

> ### SOUND BITES
> When a dog bites, there is always a good reason for his doing so. Many dogs are trained to protect a person, an area or an object. When that person, area or object is violated, the dog will attack. A dog attacks with his mouth. He has no other means of attack.
>
> Fighting dogs (and there are many breeds which fight) are taught to fight, but they also have a natural instinct to fight. This instinct is normally reserved for other dogs, though unfortunate accidents can occur; for example, when a baby crawls toward a fighting dog and the dog mistakes the crawling child as a potential attacker.
>
> If a dog is a biter for seemingly no reason, if he bites the hand that feeds him or if he snaps at members of your family, see your veterinarian or behaviorist immediately to learn how to modify the dog's behavior.

Whether you share your life with a male or a female Westie, there are certain sex-related behaviors that either sex exhibits. Spaying and neutering reduces most of these potential problems.

scolding is necessary now and then, but the focus in your training should always be on positive reinforcement.

SEXUAL BEHAVIOR

Dogs exhibit certain sexual behaviors that may have influenced your choice of male or female when you first purchased your West Highland White Terrier. Spaying/neutering will eliminate these behaviors, but if you are purchasing a dog that you wish to breed, you should be aware of what you will have to deal with throughout the dog's life.

Female dogs usually have two

A BAN ON KISSING

We all love our dogs and our dogs love us. They show their love and affection by licking us. This is not a

very sanitary practice as dogs lick and sniff in some unsavory places. Kissing your dog on the mouth is not advised, as parasites can be transmitted in this manner.

estruses per year with each season lasting about three weeks. These are the only times in which a female dog will mate and she usually will not allow this until the second week of the cycle. If a bitch is not bred during the heat cycle, it is not uncommon for her to experience a false pregnancy, in which her mammary glands swell and she exhibits maternal tendencies toward toys or other objects.

Owners must further recognize that mounting is not merely a sexual expression but also one of dominance seen in males and females alike. Be consistent and persistent and you will find that you can "move mounters."

CHEWING

The national canine pastime is chewing! Every dog loves to sink his "canines" into a tasty bone, or sometimes, whatever's within his reach. Dogs need to chew, to massage their gums, to make their new teeth feel better and to exercise their jaws. This is a natural behavior deeply imbedded in all things canine. Our role as owners is not to stop chewing, but to redirect it to positive, chew-worthy objects. Be an informed owner and purchase proper chew toys like strong nylon bones made for active dogs like your Westie. Be sure that the devices are safe and durable, since your dog's safety is at risk. Again, the owner is responsible for ensuring a dog-proof environment. The best answer is prevention: that is, put your shoes, handbags and other tasty objects in their proper places (out of the reach of the growing canine mouth). Direct puppies to their toys whenever you see them tasting the

TOO MUCH GUSTO

Males, whether castrated or not, will mount almost anything: a pillow, your leg or, much to your horror, even your neighbor's leg. As with other types of inappropriate behavior, the dog must be corrected while in the act, which for once is not difficult. Often he will not let go! While a puppy is experimenting with his very first urges, his owners feel he needs to "sow his oats" and allow the pup to mount. As the pup grows into a full-size dog, with full-size urges, it becomes a nuisance and an embarrassment. Males always appear as if they are trying to "save the race," more determined and stronger than imaginable. While altering the dog at an appropriate age will limit the dog's desire, it usually does not remove it entirely.

Chewing is as natural to a dog as breathing and barking! These puppies are "attacking" some new chew toys that are made safe for dogs.

furniture legs or your pant leg. Make a loud noise to attract the pup's attention and immediately escort him to his chew toy and engage him with the toy for at least four minutes, praising and encouraging him all the while.

A JUMP AHEAD

Stop a dog from jumping before he jumps. If he is getting ready to jump up on you, simply walk away. If he jumps on you before you can turn away, lift your knee so that it bumps him in the chest. Do not be forceful. Your dog will realize that jumping up is not a productive way of getting attention.

Some trainers recommend deterrents, such as hot pepper or another bitter spice or a product designed for this purpose, to discourage the dog from chewing unwanted objects. This is sometimes reliable, though not as often as the manufacturers of such products claim. Test out the product with your own dog before investing in large quantities.

JUMPING UP

Jumping up is a dog's friendly way of saying hello! Some dog owners do not mind when their dogs jump up, which is fine for them. The problem arises when guests come to the house and the dog greets them in the same manner—whether they like it or not! However friendly the greeting may be, chances are your visitors will not appreciate such enthusiasm from your boisterous West Highland White Terrier. The dog will not be able to distinguish upon whom he can jump and whom he cannot. Therefore, it is probably best to discourage this behavior entirely.

Pick a command such as "Off" (avoid using "Down" since you will use that for the dog to lie down) and tell him "Off" when he jumps up. Place him on the

Even a well-trained Westie may jump up on you (with his dirty feet) if he is happy to see you.

ground on all fours and have him sit, praising him the whole time. Always lavish him with praise and petting when he is in the sit position. That way you are still giving him a warm affectionate greeting, because you are as excited to see him as he is to see you!

DIGGING

Digging, which is seen as a destructive behavior to humans, is actually quite a natural behavior in dogs, especially terriers—the earth dogs! A Westie's desire to dig can be irrepressible and most frustrating to his owners, who have to bathe him every time he hits the mud! When digging occurs in your yard, it is actually a normal behavior redirected into something the dog can do in his everyday life. In the wild, a dog would be actively seeking food, making his own shelter, etc. He would be using his paws in a purposeful manner for his survival. Since you provide him with food and shelter, he has no need to use his paws for these purposes, and so the energy that he would be using manifests itself in the form of little holes all over your yard and flower beds.

Perhaps your dog is digging as a reaction to boredom—it is somewhat similar to someone eating a whole bag of chips in front of the TV—because they are there and there is not anything

> **WARNING SIGNS**
>
> If your dog barks or growls at strangers, or growls at anyone coming near his food while he is eating, playing with a toy or taking a rest in his favorite spot, he needs proper professional training because sooner or later this behavior can result in someone's being bitten.

better to do! Basically, the answer is to provide the dog with adequate play and exercise so that his mind and paws are occupied, and so that he feels as if he is doing something useful.

Of course, digging is easiest to control if it is stopped as soon as possible, but it is often hard to catch a dog in the act, especially if he is alone in the yard during the day. If your dog is a compulsive digger and is not easily distracted by other activities, you can designate an area on your property where it is okay for him to dig. If you catch him digging in an off-limits area of the yard, immediately bring him to the approved area and praise him for digging there. Keep a close eye on him so that you can catch him in the act—that is the only way to make him understand what is permitted and what is not. If you bring him to a hole he dug an hour ago and tell him "No," he will understand that you are not fond of holes, or dirt or flowers. If you catch him while he is stifle-deep in your tulips, that is when he will get your message.

BARKING

Dogs cannot talk—oh, what they would say if they could! Instead, barking is a dog's way of "talking." It can be somewhat frustrating because it is not always easy to tell what a dog means by his bark—is he excited, happy, frightened or angry? Whatever it is that the dog is trying to say, he should not be punished for barking. Only when the barking becomes excessive, and when the excessive barking becomes a bad habit, does the behavior need to be modified.

Terriers tend to be a bit barky,

Training your photogenic Westie to respect the daffodils is quite a difficult task. It's best to keep your terrier away from your flower beds!

THE "DOG IN CHARGE"

Barking is your dog's way of protecting you. If he barks at a stranger walking past your house, a moving car or a fleeing cat, he is merely exercising his responsibility to protect his pack (you) and territory from a perceived intruder. Since the "intruder" usually keeps going, the dog thinks his barking chased it away and he feels fulfilled. This behavior leads your overly vocal friend to believe that he is the "dog in charge."

---

though Westies tend to bark more purposefully than the other terriers. If an intruder came into your home in the middle of the night and your West Highland White Terrier barked a warning, you would be pleased. You would probably deem your dog a hero, a wonderful guardian and protector of the home. Barking at every outdoor noise, however, may not be welcome. For instance, if a friend drops by unexpectedly and rings the doorbell and is greeted with a sudden sharp bark, you would probably be annoyed at the dog. But in reality, this is the very same behavior that pleased you earlier. The dog does not know any better...unless he sees who is at the door and it is someone he knows, he will bark as a means of vocalizing that his (and your) territory is being threatened. While your friend is not posing a threat, it is all the same to the dog. Barking is his means of letting you know that there is an intrusion, whether friend or foe, on your property. This type of barking is instinctive and should not be discouraged.

Excessive habitual barking, however, is a problem that should be corrected early on. As your Westie grows up, you will be able to tell when his barking is purposeful and when it is for no reason; you will be able to distinguish your dog's different barks and their meanings. For example, the bark when someone comes to the door will be different from the bark when he is excited to see you. It is similar to a person's tone of voice, except that the dog has to rely totally on tone of voice because he does not have the benefit of using words. An incessant barker will be evident at an early age.

There are some things that encourage a dog to bark. For example, if your dog barks non-stop for a few minutes and you give him a treat to quiet him, he believes that you are rewarding him for barking. He will associate barking with getting a treat and will keep doing it until he is rewarded.

FOOD STEALING

Is your dog devising ways of stealing food from your pantry? If so, you must answer the following questions: Is your West Highland White Terrier hungry, or is he "constantly famished" like every

> ### "QUIET" ON THE SET
> To encourage proper barking, you can teach your dog the command "quiet." When someone comes to the door and the dog barks a few times, praise him. Talk to him soothingly and when he stops barking, tell him "Quiet" and continue to praise him. In this sense you are letting him bark his warning, which is an instinctive behavior, and then rewarding him for being quiet after a few barks.

other chow hound? Why is there food on the counter top? Face it, some dogs are more food-motivated than others. Some dogs are totally obsessed by a slab of brisket and can only think of their next meal. Food stealing is terrific fun and always yields a great reward—*food,* glorious food.

The owner's goal, therefore, is to make the "reward" less rewarding, even startling! Plant a shaker can (an empty soda can with coins inside) on the counter so that it catches your pooch off-guard. There are other devices available that will surprise the dog when he is looking for a mid-afternoon snack. Such remote-control devices, though not the first choice of some trainers, allow the correction to come from the object instead of the owner. These devices are also useful to keep the snacking hound from napping on furniture that is forbidden.

BEGGING

Just like food stealing, begging is a favorite pastime of hungry puppies! It yields that same terrific reward—*food!* Dogs quickly learn that their owners keep the "good food" for themselves, and that we humans do not dine on kibble alone. Begging is a conditioned response related to a specific stimulus, time and place. The sounds of the kitchen—cans and bottles opening, crinkling bags, the smell of food in preparation, etc.—will excite the chow hound and soon the paws are in the air!

Here is the solution to stopping this behavior: Never give in to a beggar! You are rewarding the dog for sitting pretty, jumping up, whining and rubbing his nose into you by giving him that glorious reward—food. By ignoring the dog, you will

(eventually) force the behavior into extinction. Note that the behavior likely gets worse before it disappears, so be sure there are not any "softies" in the family who will give in to little "Oliver" every time he whimpers, "More, please."

SEPARATION ANXIETY

Your West Highland White Terrier may howl, whine or otherwise vocalize his displeasure at your leaving the house and his being left alone. This is a normal case of separation anxiety and there are things that can be done to eliminate this problem. Your dog needs to learn that he will be fine on his own for a while and that he will not wither away if he is not attended to every minute of the day. In fact, constant attention can lead to separation anxiety in the first place. If you are endlessly coddling and cooing over your dog, he will come to expect this from you all of the time and it

Stealing and begging are unattractive habits in any dog. Your Westie must understand the house rules from early puppyhood, or else your adult might take over your home (and office).

> ### YOUR HOMECOMING!
> Dogs left alone for varying lengths of time may often react wildly when you return. Sometimes they run, jump, bite, chew, tear things apart, wet themselves, gobble their food or behave in other undisciplined manners. Allow them to calm down before greeting them or they will consider your attention as a reward for their antics.

will be more traumatic for him when you are not there. Obviously, you enjoy spending time with your dog and he thrives on your love and attention. However, it should not become a dependent relationship where he is heartbroken without you.

One thing you can do to minimize separation anxiety is to make your entrances and exits as low-key as possible. Do not give your dog a long drawn-out goodbye and do not lavish him with hugs and kisses when you return. This is giving in to the attention that he craves, and it will only make him miss it more when you are away. Another thing you can try is to give your dog a treat when you leave; this will not only keep him occupied and keep his mind off the fact that you just left, but it will also help him associate your leaving with a pleasant experience.

AGE OF ANXIETY
The number of dogs who suffer from separation anxiety is on the rise as more and more pet owners find themselves at work all day. New attention is being paid to this problem, which is especially hard to diagnose since it is only evident when the dog is alone. Research is currently being done to help educate dog owners about separation anxiety and about how they can help minimize this problem in their dogs.

You may have to accustom your dog to being left alone in intervals, much like when you introduced your pup to his crate. Of course, when your dog starts whimpering as you approach the door, your first instinct will be to run to him and comfort him, but do not do it! Really—eventually he will adjust and be just fine if you take it in small steps. His anxiety stems from being placed in an unfamiliar situation; by familiarizing him with being alone, he will learn that he is okay. That is not to say you should purposely leave your dog home alone, but the dog needs to know that while he can depend on you for his care, you do not have to be by his side 24 hours a day.

When the dog is alone in the house, he should be confined to

Separation anxiety is one of a Westie's worst fears. Be sensitive to your Westie's feelings whenever you leave your home.

his crate or a designated dog-proof area of the house. This should be the area in which he sleeps and already feels comfortable so he will feel more at ease when he is alone. This is just one of the many examples in which a crate is an invaluable tool for you and your dog, and another reinforcement of why your dog should view his crate as a "happy" place, a place of his own.

PHARMACEUTICAL FIX

There are two drugs specifically designed to treat mental problems in dogs. About seven million dogs each year are destroyed because owners can no longer tolerate their dogs' behavior, according to Nicholas Dodman, a specialist in animal behavior at Tufts University in Massachusetts.

The first drug, Clomicalm, is prescribed for dogs suffering from separation anxiety, which is said to cause them to react when left alone by barking, chewing their owners' belongings, drooling copiously or defecating or urinating inside the home.

The second drug, Anipryl, is recommended for cognitive dysfunction syndrome or "old dog syndrome," a mental deterioration that comes with age. Such dogs often seem to forget that they were housebroken and where their food bowls are, and they may even fail to recognize their owners.

A tremendous human-animal bonding relationship is established with all dogs, particularly senior dogs. This precious relationship deteriorates when the dog does not recognize his master. The drug can restore the bond and make senior dogs feel more like their "old selves."

COPROPHAGIA

Feces eating is, to most humans, one of the most disgusting behaviors that their dog could engage in, yet to the dog it is perfectly normal. It is hard for us to understand why a dog would want to eat his own feces. He could be seeking certain nutrients that are missing from his diet, he could be just plain hungry or he could be attracted by the pleasing (to a dog) scent. While coprophagia most often refers to the dog eating his own feces, a dog may eat that of another animal as well if he comes across it. Dogs often find the stool of cats and horses more palatable than that of other dogs. Vets have found that diets with a low digestibility, containing relatively low levels of fiber and high levels of starch, increase coprophagia. Therefore, high-fiber diets may decrease the likelihood of dogs eating feces. Both the consistency of the stool (how firm it feels in the dog's mouth) and the presence of undigested nutrients increase the likelihood. Once the dog develops diarrhea from feces eating, it will likely quit this distasteful habit.

INDEX

My West Highland White Terrier

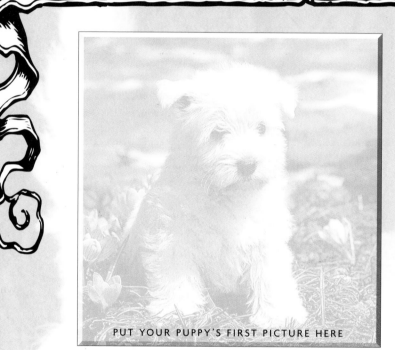

PUT YOUR PUPPY'S FIRST PICTURE HERE

Dog's Name _____

Date _____ Photographer _____